BASIC
WRITING

BASIC WRITING

Joy M. Reid
Colorado State University

Illustrations by Shelley Reid

Prentice-Hall, Inc., Englewood Cliffs, New Jersey 07632

Library of Congress Cataloging-in-Publication Data

REID, JOY M.
　　Basic writing.

　　Bibliography
　　Includes index.
　　　1. English language—Rhetoric—Problems,
exercises, etc.　2. English language—Textbooks
for foreign speakers.　I. Reid, Shelley.　II. Title.
PE1413.R36　1987　　　808′.042　　　86-30296
ISBN　0-13-069261-1

Editorial/production supervision and
　　interior design: Patricia V. Amoroso
Cover design: Karolina Harris
Manufacturing buyer: Margaret Rizzi

Printed in the United States of America

10　9　8　7　6　5　4　3　2　1

ISBN 0-13-069261-1　01

PRENTICE-HALL INTERNATIONAL (UK) LIMITED, *London*
PRENTICE-HALL OF AUSTRALIA PTY LIMITED, *Sydney*
PRENTICE-HALL CANADA INC., *Toronto*
PRENTICE-HALL HISPANOAMERICANA, S.A., *Mexico City*
PRENTICE-HALL OF INDIA PRIVATE LIMITED, *New Delhi*
PRENTICE-HALL OF JAPAN, INC., *Tokyo*
PRENTICE-HALL OF SOUTHEAST ASIA PTE. LTD., *Singapore*
EDITORA PRENTICE-HALL DO BRASIL, LTDA., *Rio de Janeiro*

Contents

2 Home 27

3 Country I 55

4 Country II 79

5 Travel Experiences 105

8 Similarities and Differences *186*

Introduction

Basic Writing is a writing text for ESL students whose English language proficiency is limited. These students are not rank beginners; rather, they form a broad group of "false beginners," students with limited English language skills, and those students whose overall proficiency is more advanced than their English writing skills. The assumption I have made about these students is that they are capable of learning (1) basic paragraph structure (a series of sentences about one idea), (2) a sense of linear sequencing, and (3) how to produce basic connectors, basic grammatical structures, and simple combined sentences.

RATIONALE

Of course, it is unreasonable to expect students who are inexperienced in both the language and the processes of written U.S. academic prose to "pick a topic and write a paragraph." However, numerous textbooks now available do focus on sentence-level grammar exercises (strings of uninteresting, unrelated, inauthentic sentences for grammatical and structural manipulation), or on one-sentence "paragraphs" and five-sentence "essays." One approach to the problem of inexperienced writers and to meeting the needs of the student-users is to consider recent ESL and native-speaker theoretical and classroom research in composing. Accordingly, I have developed the organization and the materials in *Basic Writing* in the light of four areas of research: schema theory, the "natural approach," communicative competence, and learning styles.

Schema Theory

Much schema theory research has been done exclusively in the field of ESL reading, but the results are applicable to ESL writing as well. Carrell (1983, 556) defines the basic terms: "The previously acquired knowledge is called the reader's background knowledge, and the previously acquired knowledge structures are called *schemata*. According to schema theory, comprehending a text is an interactive process between the reader's background and the text." In other words, readers understand either more or less about what they read according to what they already know. If, for example, an engineer and a psychologist read an article about cellular cofferdams, the engineer is almost certain to understand more. ESL schema theory research also considers cultural differences in rhetorical approaches. "ESL students . . . may not possess the appropriate formal schema, particularly if they come from a non-European background" (Carrell 1984, 465). A Thai student, for example, expects any general statement to come at the end of a paragraph—if at all—and therefore may find it quite strange to have to read the first sentence to determine the topic of the paragraph.

Schema theory research in reading has at least three applications to the teaching of ESL writing. First, students will have the greatest success in writing about experiences and opinions with which they are familiar. If they write about what they know and are interested in, only the language, not the content, is a barrier. Second, inexperienced writers need to accumulate background information that will provide a "framework" within which to write. Reading about the experiences and opinions of others gives the reader background about those experiences and opinions; reading expands schema, and therefore gives the readers ideas to write about. Finally, the forms of academic prose will become more accessible as students do more reading and writing; eventually, with practice and experience, the production of such prose should be easier.

In *Basic Writing* the chapters are arranged thematically, with half-a-dozen or more paragraphs about single topics (e.g., "My Family," "A Holiday in My Country") that describe common student experiences. These paragraphs have been written by international students whose writing skills are slightly to significantly more sophisticated than the basic writers who will use the text. The paragraphs, therefore, follow the general rhetorical form of U.S. academic prose, yet their content is directly relevant and available to the student readers. The paragraph topics tap the prior experiences of the readers ("Preparing for a Trip," "My Country's Flag") and present their opinions ("What Surprised Me About the United States," "What I Miss About My Country"). In addition, reading the paragraphs gives the students basic vocabulary, general background, and grammatical structures for their own paragraphs.

In addition to the thematically organized chapters, nontext materials reflect concepts and skills pertinent to U.S. academic prose. Line drawings, photographs, charts, and maps, as well as surveys and questionnaires, emerge from the themes of the chapters. These materials are designed to appeal to, and to provide practice for, the students in preacademic writing tasks: explaining, describing, discussing, and analyzing. They encourage the students to solve problems, seek advice, and draw conclusions.

The Natural Approach

Stephen Krashen and Tracy Terrell's book, *The Natural Approach* (1983), offered teachers of basic students some fresh perspectives about fulfilling the multiple needs of their students. Among their ideas is the "input hypothesis": students "acquire . . . language by understanding input that is a little beyond [their] current level of . . . competence . . . through context . . ." (32). *Basic Writing* offers students a variety of small challenges inductively, in vocabulary, grammar, and sentence structure, through student-generated paragraphs and through grammar and sentence structures that are displayed—but not explained—throughout the book. Numerous exercises that use the student paragraphs give the students ample opportunities to recognize and/or produce the displayed structures. And because the student paragraphs are authentic, without any imposed reduction in vocabulary or sentence structure (the paragraphs contain what Sandra Savignon calls a "semantically rich environment" [1983, 89]), student-users will read (and possibly produce) some rather sophisticated structures. In addition, students will have many opportunities to practice simpler structures and vocabulary, gradually improving their linguistic as well as their communicative competence.

Communicative Competence

Savignon focuses the meaning of the much misused term *communicative competence* as teaching with the emphasis on information and successful communication: "the interpretation of meaning in a context that includes shared experiences and activities of the participants" (1983, 102). The cultural component of *Basic Writing* has as its major objective the communication of shared experiences. Too often we think of international students (as opposed to native speakers) as a rather homogeneous group. However, for many basic students, often new to the language and the culture, everything and everyone (even their classmates) are *foreign*. The paragraphs in *Basic Writing* give the student-readers insights into other cultures, but more important, the students read about experiences that they can share: homesickness, culture shock, choosing a major, adjustments to the United States. For students already in the United States, the response to these paragraphs is often a relieved sigh of "me too"; the limited language proficiency of such students often makes their initial problems in the United States seem more isolated and therefore more severe. The sharing of experiences in *Basic Writing's* paragraphs and in the "interview" assignments allows the students to identify with their peers and so lessen what Krashen calls the "affective filter" (1983, 38), the closing off of paths of learning when emotional and/or intellectual overload occurs. For students not yet in the United States, the paragraphs in *Basic Writing* provide contexts, expectations, and perspectives that raise their awareness of, and enable them to prepare for, their coming experiences.

Another aspect of communicative language teaching concentrates on reality: authentic materials that focus not on learning English as a language but on "*how to do things in [English]*" (Savignon 1983, 66). This premise dictates that students must read and write for a purpose, that they should "practice with attention to the outcome" (Savignon 1983, 66). *Basic Writing* motivates students towards "real" writing by providing specific audiences for their writing: one classmate, the whole class, or, in the case of the writing projects at the end of each chapter, audiences outside the classroom, such as incoming international students, U.S. public school students, public libraries, university housing offices, etc. Moreover, students learn to write by writing, not by studying how to write; this learning-by-doing approach leads to marked improvement. The underlying philosophy of the material is to display and then to demonstrate for the students appropriate methods for communicating ideas in English; the assignments provide them with practice. Thus the objective is not to elicit sentence-level grammar structures but to discuss subject matter satisfactorily.

Learning Styles

Research in how ESL students learn best is still in its infancy, but a recent questionnaire administered to twelve hundred ESL students in intensive English language programs shows that students learn in many different ways: visually, kinesthetically, in groups or individually, etc. (Reid 1986). Other research in the cognitive development of native writers suggests that students learn at different paces and in different rhythms. Moreover, ESL learning strategies are influenced by "a wide range of factors, including aptitude, motivation, and cultural background" (Oxford-Carpenter 1985). In short, developmental skills and rates of progress differ. Some ESL students learn more successfully by studying rules and gradually applying them; others prefer to "risk" in learning. Furthermore, differences exist among languages, educational backgrounds, and major fields. Clearly, teachers need to become more sensitive to the learning strategies of students in order to determine "to what extent students' language difficulties are due to a limited or inappropriately applied repertoire of strategies" (Wenden 1985).

Given all these variables, in addition to the diversity of language proficiencies within a basic writing class, a writing textbook must allow for the wide scope of student interests, approaches to materials, and learning strategies. In *Basic Writing*, the displayed grammar and sentence structures allow the "rule-learners" to recall the rule and apply it, for example, while the "riskers" will experiment. In addition, the paragraph assignments permit different levels of response. Students who lack confidence can write more "controlled" paragraphs that are close to parts of one or more of the model paragraphs (actually, these controlled paragraphs are more like writing-readiness activities). As these students expand their vocabulary and feel more comfortable, they will branch out into more original work. More confident writers, writers who willingly take risks in their writing, and writers who are genuinely interested in and stimulated by the topic can create original paragraphs.

CONCLUSION

The most surprising lesson I learned while writing and class testing this manuscript was how much, not how little, interested students can accomplish. When I first began putting the book together, I tended to underestimate the students at every turn, despite the fact that I had been teaching ESL and basic students regularly for twenty years. My experiences with these students have shown me that the materials I have used for many, many years—primarily grammar-based texts that focused on sentence writing—while comfortable for the students, did not sufficiently motivate or challenge them. My basic students, given interesting topics, the paragraphs written by students who studied English writing before them, and opportunities to communicate directly with a variety of audiences, have produced enormous quantities of written material that has in most cases been of high quality.

Finally, I write textbooks for students and teacher's manuals for teachers. The teacher's manual for *Basic Writing* contains articles, suggestions for teaching, and approaches for helping students investigate their prewriting strategies; in addition, it contains activities for teaching paragraph revision, as well as more student paragraphs for testing and exercises.

REFERENCES

CARRELL, PATRICIA. 1983. Schema theory and ESL reading pedagogy. *TESOL Quarterly* 17(4):553–573.

————. 1984. The effects of rhetorical organization on ESL readers. *TESOL Quarterly* 18(3):441–469.

KRASHEN, STEPHEN AND TRACY TERRELL. 1983. *Language Acquisition in the Classroom*. San Francisco: The Alemany Press.

OXFORD-CARPENTER, REBECCA. 1985. Second language learning strategies: what the research has to say. *ERIC/CLL News Bulletin* 9(1): 1–5.

REID, JOY. 1986. Learning styles of ESL students. *TESOL Quarterly* 20(3).

SAVIGNON, SANDRA. 1983. *Communicative Competence: Theory and Classroom Practice*. Rowley, Mass.: Addison-Wesley.

WENDEN, ANITA. 1985. Learner strategies. *TESOL Newsletter* xix(5):1, 5.

ACKNOWLEDGMENTS

Many people deserve thanks for their help with *Basic Writing*. Mary Jane Peluso at Macmillan generously sent me helpful reviews from Ilona Leki (University of Tennessee), and Martha Pennington (University of Hawaii).

Prentice-Hall reviewers Gloria Bliss, Betsy Soden, Jill Brand, and Maryann O'Brien also provided me with advice and suggestions. Teachers in the Colorado State University Intensive English Program who class-tested the materials and gave valuable feedback included Celeste Lasky, Judy Solanki, Mark Mancosky, Larry Smith, and Susan Parks. Finally, I thank my production editor at Prentice-Hall, Patricia Amoroso, whose careful editing and commitment to quality improved the textbook.

My special thanks to Shelley Reid, who drew the illustrations and helped with the production of *Basic Writing*; to Peggy Lindstrom and Eloise Ariza, who willingly gave their time, energy, and ideas; to my students, who eagerly donated their writing samples for use in the book; to U.S. teachers abroad who wrote me of their experiences; and to Steve and Michael, who gave me their patience and support.

BASIC
WRITING

One

Family

My Mother

I would like to write about the relationship between my mother and me. My mother is the person who has influenced me for more than twenty years. She is a beautiful woman, and she taught me principles of what is good and what is bad. She also told me about her religion. Now I am twenty years old, and I understand why she was strict with me. When I have a problem now, I call my mother because she is still the person who takes care of me.

Erich Backhoff
Mexico

TO BE

Present (now)		*Past (yesterday)*	
I	am	I	was
he she it	is	he she it	was
we you they	are	we you they	were

___ EXERCISE 1A _____

Underline the verb TO BE in the following paragraph.

My Family

My father was born in Honduras, and my mother is from Mexico. There are eight children in my family, seven sons and me. I have two married brothers, and each brother has a daughter. My oldest brother is a civil engineer, and my other brother is an agronomy engineer. Also, I have two brothers studying in a technical college in Monterrey, Mexico. My two younger brothers are studying in high school in Honduras.

Maria Guadalupe Gabrie
Honduras

Write the TO BE verbs in the paragraph below.

My Sister and Brothers

My sister's name _____ Marta. She _____ twenty years old. She _____ married, and she has two daughters. She _____ a doctor, and she lives in Portugal. I have two brothers. Their names _____ Leonel and Alcino. They _____ thirty-two and twenty-four years old. Leonel lives in Keene, Texas. Alcino lives in S. Tomé. They _____ married, but they do not have any children. Leonel _____ a businessman, and Alcino _____ a teacher.

Semoa de Sousa
Sao Tomé, West Africa

The Mother

The grass grows because of the spring sun,
but the grass can't give anything back to the sun in return.
It is the same with mother's love.
The love is so great and deep that a son, like inch-long grass,
can hardly return his mother's love.
How much love can the inch-long grass
give to the spring sun in return?

translated by
Prayat Laoprafossone
Thailand

TO HAVE

	Present (now)		Past (yesterday)	
I	have	I	had
he she it	has	he she it	had
you we they	have	you we they	had

My Large Family

    I <u>HAVE</u> a large family. They are in Venezuela. My family <u>HAS</u> ten people: my father, my mother, five sisters, two brothers, and me. My father <u>HAS</u> three brothers, and my mother <u>HAS</u> three sisters and one brother. All my uncles and my aunts live in Maracaibo City, but my family lives in Caracas. My father is 62 years old, and my mother is 54 years old. My father <u>HAS</u> a job at the Occidental Bank. He is a statistics supervisor. My mother doesn't work now, but she was a teacher and a director at the high school. I <u>HAVE</u> many cousins because my aunts and uncles are all married. My sisters are married too, and they <u>HAVE</u> many children. For example, my first sister is a doctor, and she <u>HAS</u> a child. My second sister is a dentist, and she <u>HAS</u> two children, one boy and one girl. My third sister is a doctor, and she <u>HAS</u> three children, two boys and one girl. My fourth and fifth sisters do not <u>HAVE</u> any children because they are not married.

José Ochea
Venezuela

—— EXERCISE 1C ——————————————

Write the TO HAVE verbs in the paragraph below.

My Brother

    My brother Evaristo is a special person in my life. He has helped me

since I was born. He was always a good student and tried to be an

example for my brothers and me. He was always number one in all

sports, and for that reason we wanted to be like him. Now he

_____ a good job in a good company, and in a few years he is going to work for himself. He _____ a big truck, and he will use it to transport iron pipes around Mexico. He got married one-and-a-half years ago, and now he _____ a good wife and a baby. They live in a good neighborhood with most of their friends close to their house. I _____ a special feeling for my brother because he _____ always taken care of me.

Marcelo Mendez
Mexico

Make new friends, but also keep old friends.
One is silver, the other is gold.
All of them are just like jewels.
Age will mellow and refine them.

translated by
Saud Degel
Saudi Arabia

POSSESSIVE ADJECTIVES

My mother	*His* father's name
Her sister's children	*Our* brother
Your cousin	*Their* parents

My Mother

MY mother's name is Maria de los Angeles Ramirez Enriquez. She is 52 years old, and she has black hair and brown eyes the same as mine. HER first name, Maria, has a Catholic meaning. In Mexico it is a very common custom to use the names Maria and Guadalupe for women. MY mother's birthplace was Veracruz, a tropical state in Mexico that is close to the Gulf of Mexico. Now MY mother's home is in Mexico City, and she is a teacher in a primary school.

Raymundo Iturbe
Mexico

Read the paragraphs that follow. Write the TO BE verbs in the blanks. <u>Underline</u> the possessive adjectives.

I

My Cousins

My three cousins and their families live in the U.S. Leonor, my oldest cousin, _____ 30 years old. She lives with her mother (my aunt) in a beautiful home in Washington D.C. Leonor's brother _____ named German. He _____ a Catholic priest, and he made the celebration of my marriage. His church _____ in New York City. Oscar _____ my other cousin. He lives with his family in their large house in Houston, Texas. His daughter's name _____ Janet, and his son's name _____ Miguel.

Misela Marquez
Venezuela

II

My Father

My father _____ important in my life. All these years he has been my friend. When I _____ a small boy, he took me to my school. I _____ not afraid, and I learned as much as I could. All these years, his love for me has helped me in difficult moments. He has been beside me, telling me what to do. This year, I _____ in the U.S., and I _____ going to study administration because my father wants me to study. In the future, I will return to my home, and I will work there with my father.

Santiago Mendez
Venezuela

> The duck's son is a swimmer.
>
> translated by
> *Youssef El-Tayash*
> Libya

QUESTIONS

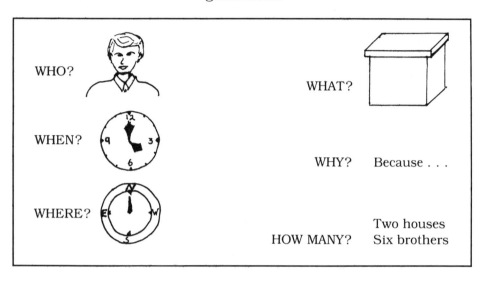

WHO?

WHEN?

WHERE?

WHAT?

WHY?   Because . . .

Two houses
HOW MANY?   Six brothers

___ **WRITING ASSIGNMENT** _____

*Look at the photograph on page 8. Read the information about
the family. Then complete the paragraph that follows. Write the
correct form of the verbs TO BE and TO HAVE in the blanks.
Write the correct possessive adjective in the other blanks.*

Moussa's Family

This _____ a picture of Moussa's family. Moussa
     be

_____ the father. He _____ not in the photo.
be   **be**

Moussa's wife's name _____ Fati Mouss. She
           be

_____ 24 years old. Moussa _____ three
be   have

children. _____ older son _____ 5 years old.
                                be

Yacoubor is _____ name. Moussa's younger son

_____ 3 years old. _____ name _____
be   be

Issaka. Moussa's daughter _____ 3 years old. _____
be

name _____ Kadi. Moussa and _____ family
be

_____ from Niger.
be

Moussa Hossane's Family from Niger

Older son: Yacoubor Hossane (5 years old)
Younger son: Issaka Hossane (2 years old)
Daughter: Kadi Hossane (3 years old)
Wife: Fati Mouss (24 years old)

Subject	Object
I	me
you	you
he, she, it	him, her, it
we	us
you	you
they	them
this	those

___ EXERCISE 1E _____

Read the paragraph below. If Abdullah wrote the paragraph, he would use "I," "my," and "me." If his friend Ali writes the paragraph about Abdullah, Ali will use "he," "his," and "him."

My (His) Mother

My / His mother is someone inside me. / him. I / He can never forget her. She died, but she is both a sadness and an unforgettable smile in my / his life. She is a sadness because I / he lost her, and she is a smile because she taught me / him so many things about life and people. I / He can never forget her because she taught me / him the meaning of strength and mercy. She was very strong with me / him whenever I / he did something wrong. But she was very merciful when she saw me / him in a bad mood or when I / he was sick. I / He could always see love in her eyes.

Abdullah Amirah
Saudi Arabia

Read the paragraphs on page 10. Then do the exercises that follow.

I

My Mother

I will tell you something about my mother. My mother's name is Lourdes Moncada. She is from Spain, but she has lived in Nicaragua, her husband's country, for 23 years. She is a tender woman. For example, when my sister and I are sleeping, she comes into our room, no matter what the hour, and she kisses us. She does the same thing every night. My mother helps people wherever they need her. One day, a poor boy came to our home with a big wound on his arm, and my mother cured him. However, when she gets angry, she really does. Last year my brother broke a living room lamp, and she made him buy a new one with his own money. Right now she is living in a small town with my father and her children.

Maria Lourdes Moncada
Nicaragua

—— EXERCISE 1F ——————————————————————

1. Underline the subject pronouns in the paragraph above.
2. Circle 6 possessive adjectives in the paragraph.
3. Where was Maria's mother born?
4. How many times does Maria use the word "mother" in this paragraph?

II

My Mother's Feet

My mother, even though she is a normal mother, has something different from other mothers: her feet. Do not think that my mother is a monster. No! The difference is that my mother's feet are generally bigger than other mothers' feet, at least in my country. For example, when my mother goes to a shoe store in Colombia, she cannot find her size, which is usually bigger than the biggest shoe in the store. So, sometimes my mother's feet are a problem, not only for her, but also for me. The other day I had to buy a pair of "nice" shoes here in the United States to send to her. The problem was whether the shoes I chose were "nice" or not. They seemed nice to me, but I do not know if she really liked them. Usually my mother has to wait for nearly a month for her new shoes from the United States or from the factory. I tell my mother that she has "American feet."

Jorge Ramirez
Colombia

1. <u>Underline</u> 5 subject pronouns in paragraph II.
2. (Circle) 5 possessive adjectives in the paragraph.
3. Why does Jorge buy shoes for his mother in the United States?
4. Write this paragraph about Jorgé's mother again. Use "he," "his," and "him" instead of "I," "my," and "me."

WRITING ASSIGNMENT

Write the answers to the following questions about your family.

What is your father's name?

How old is your father?

What is your father's job?

What is your mother's name?

What is your mother's job?

Where do your parents live?

How many sisters do you have?

What are their names?

How old are they?

How many brothers do you have?

What are their names?

How old are they?

The Rose (a children's poem)

From the sky a rose fell down.
My grandmother picked it up.
She wore it on her head,
And how nice it was to look at.

translated by
John Shyh-Yuan Wang
China (P.R.C.)

Capitalize:

the first letter of each sentence
the first letter of the names of people, cities, countries
the first letter of each word in a title
the pronoun "I"

My Grandfather

My grandfather is the head of my family. His name is Tarik, the same as mine, and he is the oldest man in my family. He is smart, strong, and wise. He was a member of the Iraqi revolution against the English enemies during the First World War. He has lived a simple life with no cars, electricity, or television. When he was a young man, he traveled by horse, by camel, and by small boat. He needed strong nerves. Now he stays at our home,and he advises us.

Tarik Swadi Abdulsada
Iraq

___ EXERCISE 1H _____

Capitalize the appropriate words in the following paragraph. In the paragraph, 17 letters need to be capitalized.

---

my grandmother

My grandmother is different from me. she is short and fat and very white, but i am tall and thin and darker. she is beautiful, but i am not. her name is mahvash. she has a small view of the world because she is not well educated. for example, she does not know that other parts of the world have different types of lives and different religions. she never tries to learn new things. she is satisfied with her life in iran.

parvin safari
iran

A good neighbor is better than a brother who is far away.

translated by
Kyu-Yong Lee
Korea

SUBJECT—VERB—COMPLEMENT

Subject	Verb	Complement
My mother	is	a traditional Chinese woman.
She	is	honest, hard-working, and patient.
She	has	black hair and brown eyes.
My father	needs	her every day.
Mother	encourages	her children to be courageous.
She	lives	in Taiwan with her family.
My mother	is	my teacher and my friend.

Julie Li-Chu Chung
Taiwan (R.O.C.)

Read the paragraphs below. Circle the subject (S) *in each underlined sentence. Circle the verb* (V) *in each sentence. Then do the exercises that follow each paragraph.*

I

My Father

My father is the strongest person in our family, but he also has kindness and wisdom. He was born at the beginning of the century. He grew up in a very hard environment. As I grew up, I knew my father as a very loving and generous man. He taught us to be very polite. He encouraged our good behavior and good feelings toward each other. He believed that every one of his sons should be a man in his appearance and his behavior.

Ahmed Ghamdy
Saudi Arabia

1. Put brackets [   ] around the possessive adjectives in the paragraph.
2. What is this paragraph about?
3. When was Ahmed's father born?
4. How many times does Ahmed use the word "father" in this paragraph?

II

My Father

The most important person in my life is my father. He has been the example for me to develop my social and professional life. In my social life, he showed me how to be with people and what behavior I need to have in different situations. For example, I talk or behave differently with a director of a company than with a worker. My father could not study in school, but he has a lot of experience. He is a good worker with high responsibilities in his work. He also taught me that the most important responsibilities are to my work and my family. My father was a very good baseball player when he was young. He likes all sports, and he taught me to play sports with a clear mind. My father is an average person. However, he has been the biggest person for me.

Juan Manuel Ortiz Mata
Mexico

—— EXERCISE 1J ————————————————————————

1. Circle the subject (S) and the verb (V) of each underlined sentence.
2. Put parentheses (   ) around 5 subject pronouns.
3. Put brackets [   ] around 5 possessive adjectives.
4. What has Juan learned from his father?

III

Thrifty Mother

My mother is very thrifty, and that _____ very important

for our family happiness. If my mother wants to buy something, usually

she checks the prices from several places before she decides where she wants to shop. Sometimes the difference of the price _____ not too much, but she likes to spend her time bargaining. <u>By doing that, my mother saves some of her daily expenses.</u> On special occasions, like birthdays, my mother can make a special party without asking for additional money from my father. When my father _____ not at home, my mother can solve unexpected problems by using her savings from daily expenses. <u>For example, sometimes our family needs extra money to go to the doctor or to buy medicine.</u> My mother's thrifty ways _____ helpful for all of my family.

Juliardi Kahar
Indonesia

___ EXERCISE 1K _____

1. Write the correct verb TO BE in the blanks.
2. Circle the subject Ⓢ and the verb Ⓥ in the <u>underlined</u> sentences.
3. Can you guess the meaning of "thrifty" from the underlined sentences in the paragraph?
4. Why is Juliardi's mother "special"?

THE PARAGRAPH

Title

(indent)

--------▶ A paragraph is a group of sentences about ONE MAIN IDEA. Usually the title and the first sentence of the paragraph tell the main idea of the paragraph. The first sentence of the paragraph is indented. Each sentence in the paragraph begins with a capital letter. All the sentences in the paragraph have a subject and a verb. Each sentence ends with a period (.).

Look at the photograph below. Write a paragraph about the photo. Answer some of the following questions:

How many people are in the family?

How many children are in the family?

How many sons?

How old are the people in the family?

What are the names of the people in the family?

Where is the family from?

The Family of Ryu Ki Hee from Korea

Father: Ryu Ki Hee (32 years old)
Mother: Park Jung Sook (31 years old)
Older son: Ryu Dae Kue (7 years old)
Younger son: Ryu Shin Kue (6 years old)

Read the paragraphs on page 17. Then do the exercises that follow.

I

My Cousin

My best friend is named Federico, and he is also my cousin. Federico and I are the same age, but he is taller than I am. <u>He has dark, curly hair and blue eyes.</u> We studied together in elementary school, in high school, and at the same university. We spent much time together, talking about problems in our lives. <u>We never had a fight.</u> <u>We always tried to help each other.</u> In high school, we enjoyed playing a sport called *toros coleados* which is practiced with horses and bulls. <u>Federico is also a good guitar player.</u> Now, when I hear someone playing a guitar, I think of my good friend.

Mario Martinez
Venezuela

___ EXERCISE 1L _____

1. Circle the subject (S) in the underlined sentences.
2. Put the verb (V) in parentheses in the underlined sentences.
3. Why does Mario like Federico?
4. Why does Mario think about Federico when he hears guitar music?

II

My Mother's Cooking

When I lived at home, I loved the delicious food my mother fixed. She is interested in fixing a traditional food called upside-downs. The food contains meat and rice and potatoes. It _____ a good smell and taste, and I could smell it from a long distance. I could pick the dish my mother fixed from many other dishes because she _____ special experience. In addition, she always makes noises when she prepares the food, like the noise of the spoons and dishes. When I heard that noise, I became impatient and hungry. As long as I was at home, I never missed my mother's food. But now I miss it every day. I will always remember my mother's food as long as I live.

Basem Masaedeh
Saudi Arabia

1. What is the main idea of this paragraph?
2. Draw the arrow (-----▶) to show the indentation of the first sentence of the paragraph.
3. Write the correct verb TO HAVE in the blanks.
4. Circle the period at the end of each sentence.

_____ **WRITING ASSIGNMENT** _____

Answer the questions below. Write a paragraph about ONE special person in your family (your mother? your cousin? your brother? your grandfather?).

Who is the person?

What does he or she look like?

How old is he or she?

Why are you writing about this person?

What makes this person "special"?

Has the person influenced you? In what ways?

Use the chart below to help plan your paragraph.

Adjectives	*How do you know?*
warm, loving	She smiles a lot.
understanding	He listens to my problems.
helpful	She tries to help her friends.
young	_____
generous	_____
_____	_____
_____	_____
_____	_____

> If there is a well in a dry field,
> we will take a bath.
> If God spares our lives,
> We will meet again.
>
> translated by
> *Hadi Pasaribu*
> Indonesia

Read the paragraphs below. Then do the exercises that follow.

I

---

my first name, sakda, was the name of a man who was well-known by people in my country, thailand. In 1939 he was the only soldier who escaped from the battle with the communists in the jungle. my first name means "a man who has power and strength," so my first name is a special name in thai. my last name, wattanasupt, was given by the seventh king of thailand. in my country, most of my friends call me "aye" because thai people don't like to say long names. also, short nicknames, like aye, show the close relationship between my friends and me.

Sakda Wattanasupt
Thailand

___ EXERCISE 1N _____

1. Capitalize the appropriate words in the paragraph. 13 words need to be capitalized.
2. Write a title for this paragraph. Be sure to capitalize the first letter of each word in your title.
3. Circle 5 TO BE verbs in this paragraph.
4. Why is the writer called "Aye"?

II

Some Things About My Name

The Venezuelan people have a custom that every child be called by four names: two first names and two last names. My last names are from my mother's side and my father's side of the family. Therefore, my complete name is Hilda Zulema Gonzalez Cruz. My first name, Hilda, is the same as my mother's first name. My father wanted to give me my mother's name because I am the first and only daughter after four sons. <u>My second name, Zulema, has a curious history.</u> When my mother was pregnant, she listened to a famous novel on the radio, called *Prince Tamacun*. In this novel there were two princesses: Arelis and Zulema. My parents asked my older brother what name he preferred, Arelis or Zulema. <u>He chose Zulema.</u> <u>It is a name from Arabia.</u> Gonzalez, my third name, is very common in my country. <u>It is from my father.</u> Finally, my last name, Cruz, is from the Canary Islands. <u>This name was given to my mother's family by my great-great-grandfather.</u>

Zulema Gonzalez
Venezuela

____ EXERCISE 10 _____

1. Circle the subject Ⓢ and the verb Ⓥ in the underlined sentences.
2. Put parentheses around 8 possessive adjectives.
3. How many times does Zulema use the word "name(s)" in the paragraph?
4. Change the pronouns I and my to she and her in this paragraph.

____ INTERVIEW _____

Ask your classmate the questions below. Write the answers to the questions. Use the correct subject pronouns. Then introduce your classmate to the other people in your class.

What is your name?

What country are you from?

How old are you?

Are you married?

What is your major?

Where do you live now?

How long have you been in the U.S.?

> Do not ignore small things because they have their uses. For example, a sword is useless when a needle is needed.
>
> translated by
> *Dattatray Vaidankar*
> India

Read the paragraphs below. Then do the exercises that follow.

I

My Name

My name is Hu Cheng-Hwa. Hu is not my first name. It is my family name. The family name is first in the traditional Chinese style. In the U.S., many people are not able to pronounce my family name correctly. In Chinese, "Hu" is quite different from "Who," but the sounds in English are not different. Most people in Taiwan call me "Lau-Hu." *Lau* means "old." However, in Chinese, the meaning is not "old" when someone calls his friend "Lau." It is just for friendship. Cheng-Hwa is my given name. *Cheng* means "real," "true." *Hwa* means Chinese. So my name means "really Chinese." Of course, I am not able to write my name in the Chinese style in the U.S. Therefore, my name here is Cheng-Hwa Hu.

Cheng-Hwa Hu
Taiwan (R.O.C.)

EXERCISE 1P

1. What is the main idea of this paragraph?
2. Circle the subject (S) and the verb (V) in the underlined sentences.
3. Put brackets around 5 possessive adjectives.
4. Why can't people in the U.S. pronounce Hu's name?

II

My Name

My first name is a Spanish one: Fernando. In my country, it is traditional to choose the child's first name (or names) from among his ancestors' first names. It is also good to include the name of a saint to protect the child. A lucky child can have three or four names. I was not lucky. My brothers and cousins had used all the ancestors' names, so I did not have a saint to protect me. My mother chose Fernando because this was the name of Spanish kings. She believed that her family had very pure Spanish blood. My last name is Arango, and it is the last name of all my ancestors from my father's line. This name originated in a Spanish province called Aragon. Perhaps one foolish ancestor changed the spelling, and instead of Aragon, he wrote Arango!

Fernando Arango
Colombia

—— EXERCISE 1Q ——————————————————

1. What is the main idea of this paragraph?
2. Circle the subject Ⓢ and the verb Ⓥ in the underlined sentences.
3. Why was Fernando not "lucky"?
4. How many times does the writer use the word "name(s)"? Why?

—— **WRITING ASSIGNMENT** ——————————————

Answer the questions below. Write a paragraph about your name.

What is your complete name?

What does each of your names mean?

Why did your parents give you your name(s)?

What is special about your name?

Is there anything amusing about your name?

> If you work harder and harder, you'll get results.
>
> translated by
> *Mohamud Fahie*
> Somalia

Read the paragraphs below. Then do the exercises that follow.

I

My Name

My name is Jun Wang, Eric. Jun is my first name. Wang is my second name. Usually, a Chinese name includes three parts: first, second, and last. However, I do not have a second name. In Chinese, Jun, my first name, means "a great strong white horse who can run rapidly, 10,000 miles a day." Chinese people always use the word Jun to encourage someone to reach a goal. My last name, Wang, means "king" in Chinese. According to Chinese tradition, the hope of my future is explained by my name. Unfortunately, I found a problem when I came to the U.S. My first name was not clear to people because it is similar to June, which is a girl's name and the name of a summer month. For this reason, I have been given an American name, Eric, that also means "king."

Jun Wang
China (P.R.C.)

—— EXERCISE 1R ————————————————————

1. Circle the subject Ⓢ and the verb Ⓥ in the underlined sentences.
2. Put parentheses around the TO BE and TO HAVE verbs.
3. Why does Jun have a North American name?
4. Why was he named Eric?

II

Marysol Coromoto Rangel Martinez de Berti

Marysol, my first name, is derived from the Spanish name, Maria. This is for the Virgin Mary. In Spanish, *soledad* means "lonely." But my wonderful parents did not like that meaning. Therefore, they named me Marysol. *Mar* means "sea," and *sol* means "sun." A problem came when I was baptized because Marysol was not a religious name. So my parents also gave me the name Coromoto, after a saint who lived in the nineteenth century in Venezuela. I have three last names. The first, Rangel, is my father's. It originated in Spain, and then it became an Indian name in the Andes, the region where my father was born. My second name, Martinez, is my mother's maiden name. It also came from Spain, and afterwards from the region in Venezuela called Aragua. Finally, I have a married name. In my country, when a woman marries, she adds the term *de* and her husband's name. The *de* means she is *de*pendent on her husband. My husband's name, Berti, is from Italy, from the island of Elba. It is a name of noble origin.

Marysol Rangel de Berti
Venezuela

___ EXERCISE 1S ___

1. Circle the subject (S) and the verb (V) in the underlined sentences.
2. Put parentheses around the TO BE and TO HAVE verbs.
3. Put brackets around 6 subject pronouns.
4. What does the name Marysol mean in English?

To those who stand under a good tree, a good shadow nurtures them.

translated by
Olga Handal
Honduras

___ WRITING ASSIGNMENT ___

Look at the photographs on the next page. Choose one photograph. Write a paragraph about the family in that photograph. Answer some of the questions below.

How many people are in the family?

How many children are in the family?

How many sons? How many daughters?

What does the father look like?

What does the mother look like?

What does each child look like?

How old is each person in the family?

Where is the family from?

What are the names of the people in the family?

The Family of Bonar Siregar from Indonesia

Father: Bonar Siregar (45 years old)
Mother: N. Sitorus (42 years old)
Older son: Ivan (14 years old)
Older daughter: Imelda (13 years old)
Younger daughter: Indra (12 years old)
Younger son: Ivo (8 years old)

The Family of Hiroyuki Nakama from Japan

Father: Hiroyuki Namaka (38 years old)
Mother: Noriko Nakama (37 years old)
Older daughter: Ayano Nakama (14 years old)
Younger daughter: Hiroko Nakama (6 years old)

My Friend   My Next-Door Neighbor

My Teacher   My Sister's (Brother's) Friend

My Sister's (Brother's) Name

WRITING PROJECTS

Individual Writing Project

Write several paragraphs about the people in your family. The titles of your paragraphs might be:

My Mother   My Oldest Sister (Brother)

My Father   My Youngest Brother (Sister)

My Grandmother   My Brothers (Sisters)

My Grandfather   My Cousin(s)

In each paragraph, answer some of these questions:

What is her or her name?

Where does he or she live?

What is his or her job?

What does he or she look like?

Why is he or she special?

Is he or she married?

Is he or she studying?

What do you remember about him or her?

When you have finished the paragraphs, make a booklet. Use photographs of your family to make the booklet more interesting. Use construction paper and staples or brads to fasten the booklet together. Decorate the front of the booklet with the title and other art work. Display the booklets in your classroom, and invite another class to come to your class and read the booklets.

Group Writing Project

Ask friends who are NOT in your class to write paragraphs about their names. Or, interview several friends about their names, and write paragraphs about those names. Gather all the paragraphs written in class and by your friends. Put the paragraphs into a booklet. Make copies of the booklet for all the students who contributed paragraphs.

Two

Home

 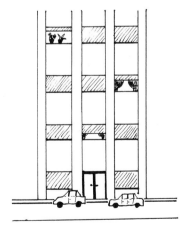

My Hometown

Alexandria is the second biggest city in my country, Egypt, and I live in this city. It is a beautiful city, and people there are very kind and polite. Tourists like to visit my city because it is on the sea. When I walk down the Kornash, the largest street, I see the beautiful blue sea and sky, and the beautiful green grass and trees. In the spring, the flowers grow in many colors: yellow, red, and blue. The most beautiful scene is the white birds. In the winter, a very big flock of birds migrates to this place. I watch them while they skillfully fish from the sea. The birds watch the fish, and they wait patiently for a long time. When the fish come to the surface, they fly quickly and catch them. In the fall, the city looks like a very old man because the leaves of the trees fall from the trees. That is my city, and I think it is the most beautiful city in the world.

Abdelmegig Fahmy
Egypt

PRESENT TENSE VERBS (every day, a habit)

Subject		Verb	Complement
I		talk	to my mother.
He — Ali *OR* Abdul		lives	in Egypt.
She — Marta *OR* Hussa		writes	letters to her friends.
It — The river *OR*		flows	through the village.
The cat		runs	across the room
You	Mahmoud and Sylvia	help	the new students.
We	Tarig, Mariana, and Kumi	come	to class every day
They	Lucas and Parvin	drink	tea at breakfast.

comes(s)	help(s)	rise(s)	stand(s)
drink(s)	is (are)	run(s)	start(s)
feel(s)	like(s)	speak(s)	think(s)
find(s)	live(s)	spend(s)	walk(s)
give(s)	put(s)	spread(s)	write(s)

Night falls, darkness spreads.
The wind, surging through the fields
Brings my thoughts home.

translated by
Sin S. Chiu
Hong Kong

My Hometown

The city I LIVE in is called Haifa. Haifa is a beautiful city with a magnificent panorama. It STARTS at the Mediterranean Sea, CONTINUES with a flat area that ENDS at the slopes of the Carmel Mountains. I LIVE about half way up the mountain, and I HAVE a beautiful view spreading below. The house I LIVE in is in an apartment building with a red roof. I LIVE on the upper floor.

Shoshana Zachs
Israel

___ EXERCISE 2A ___

Read the paragraphs on page 30. Some present tense verbs are underlined. Circle the subject for each underlined present tense verb.

I

My City

My city, Huanzheu, <u>is</u> a famous beautiful city in China, and it <u>is</u> famous all over the world too. It <u>is</u> set between the river and West Lake. Several hills <u>spread</u> around West Lake, and some mountains <u>stand</u> by the river. These <u>give</u> the city many beautiful scenes, and so Huanzheu <u>is</u> famous for its beauty. It <u>is</u> beautiful in the spring when the trees bud green and the peach trees flower with their red blossoms. It <u>is</u> beautiful in the summer when the lilies <u>float</u> in the lake. It <u>is</u> beautiful in the fall when the leaves <u>turn</u> yellow and red. And it <u>is</u> beautiful in the winter when the snow <u>gives</u> white clothes to the mountains. So Huanzheu <u>is</u> beautiful all year. It <u>is</u> beautiful when the sunshine <u>is</u> bright because the hills <u>make</u> shadows in the lake. It <u>is</u> beautiful when the rain <u>falls</u> and makes the frogs rise from the lake. My city <u>is</u> always beautiful.

Dong Aichu
China (P.R.C.)

II

My Hometown

My hometown, Chia-Yi, <u>is</u> located in southwest Taiwan. It <u>is</u> mostly surrounded by plains that produce rice, but the region also <u>grows</u> fruit. Because it <u>is</u> in a subtropical zone, it <u>produces</u> fruit all year. Mango, pineapple, and papaya <u>are</u> my favorite fruits in the summertime, and I <u>enjoy</u> oranges, grapes, and bananas during our short "winter." We can always get fresh vegetables and fruit at very reasonable prices. Because they <u>are</u> so fresh, they <u>taste</u> delicious. Now that I <u>am</u> far away from Chia-Yi, I often <u>think</u> of a Chinese poem:

> After I <u>lift</u> up my head.
> to see the brilliant moon,
> I <u>lower</u> my head
> and think of my hometown.

Chia-Chu Dorland
Taiwan (R.O.C.)

Read the paragraphs below. In each blank (_____), write the correct present tense verb.

I

My Small Town

Soba is a small town in my country, Sudan. It _____ 15

be

kilometers from Khartoum, the capital of Sudan. The Nile River

_____ through Soba. That _____ the town green

flow   **make**

and beautiful. Most of the people in Soba _____ as farmers

work

or fishermen. The Nile is very important in their lives. A small market

in Soba _____ food to the people who cannot go to the market

sell

in the capital. In Soba, a small hospital and a pharmacy _____

give

medicine to the people without money. About 50 percent of the people

in Soba _____ in the hospital. The youth club in Soba

work

_____ the youth a place to meet every night except Friday.

give

Friday _____ a holy day in Soba, so the people _____ to

be   **go**

the mosque, and they _____ their prayers. The people in Soba

say

_____ their town. They _____ very happy because

love   **be**

Soba is crowded with beautiful things.

Shiek Idris Mahmoud Hassan

Sudan

II

My Hometown

Taipei, the city where I _____, is the most beautiful
                  live

city I have ever seen. It is located among the mountains—Yun Ming

San, Chi-Sing San, Wi-Ji San, and Gun-In San—so the air around the

city _____ very fresh. Many rivers _____ through
     be   **flow**

the city, so the scenery is beautiful. The buildings _____
                                             be

traditional Chinese style. I never _____ lonely because there
                               feel

are so many places to enjoy myself. About 70 theaters, 100 galleries,

10 museums, and 5 gymnasiums, _____ the people busy. I
                                   keep

_____ Chinese food, so I _____ Taipei. There are
  like   **love**

about 3,000 Chinese restaurants there, and the food they _____
                                                   serve

is very delicious and fresh.

Chi-Chang Wang
Taiwan (R.O.C.)

___ **WRITING ASSIGNMENT** _____

*Write a paragraph about your hometown. Answer some of the
questions below.*

What is the name of your hometown?

Where is it?

How large (or how small) is it?

What does your hometown look like?

What is the weather in your hometown?

What makes your hometown beautiful?

What makes your hometown special?

PRESENT TENSE SPELLING (He, She, It + Present Tense)*

	Regular	**Verbs that end in -sh, -ch, -ss, -x**	**Verbs that end vowel + y**		**Verbs that end in consonant + y**	
	smiles	brushes	pay	pays	study	studies
	walks	washes	buy	buys	worry	worries
HE	closes	teaches			carry	carries
SHE	speaks	watches			enjoy	enjoys
IT	says	kisses				
	looks	tosses				
	drives	relaxes				
	turns					
	works					
	looks					

___ EXERCISE 2C _____

Read the following paragraphs. Choose the correct present tense verb from the list below each paragraph. Write the correct form of each present tense verb in the blank (_____). Use each verb on the list only once.

---

*See the inside front cover of this text for spelling rules.

I

Jubeal

My country, Lebanon, is all beautiful, but one city _____
more beautiful than the others. Jubeal is the small city where I
_____. On one side of the city, the golden sand of the beach
beside the sea reflects the sunlight like a colored mirror. In the summer,
people fill the beach. They _____ the sunlight, and they
_____ in the sea. Away from the sea, the mountains
_____ in the middle of the city. Their green trees and grasses
_____ the people in Jubeal happy. From these mountains, rivers
_____ into the city. The sounds of the rivers are like melodies in
heaven. All these things make Jubeal a beautiful place.

VERBS: enjoy   swim   be   make   live   rise   flow

Mustapha Ghaddar
Lebanon

II

My Hometown

I _____ that one of the most beautiful cities in my country
is Villavicencio. It _____ a typical Colombian country town. Near
the town are many farms and cows, and often the farmers _____
parties like North American rodeos. People in the town _____
Villavicencio "the door of the jungle" because the jungle is very near the
town. Many tourists _____ to Villavicencio because there are
beautiful places to visit and many things to do. For example, the Andes
Mountains _____ behind the city, and they are very beautiful.
Many rivers _____ near the city. I _____ fishing to a
different river almost every day. There are also many places for hunting
in the jungle and in the mountains.

VERBS: be   have   think   flow   call   go   rise   come

Jorge Cano
Colombia

Each year for three hundred and sixty years
the cutting wind and biting frost contend.
How long can beauty flower fresh and fair?
In a single day wind can whirl it to its end.

translated by
Xirong Wei
China (P.R.C.)

___ **WRITING ASSIGNMENT** _____

Write a paragraph about another beautiful city in your country.
Answer some of the questions below.

What is the name of the city?

Where is it located?

How large (or small) is it?

In what ways is it beautiful?

Why do you like the city?

Do you like to visit the city? Why?

THERE IS/THERE ARE

There is + (SUBJECT) + (COMPLEMENT)

There is (a beautiful park) in my hometown.

There are + (SUBJECT) + (COMPLEMENT)

There are (many parks) in my hometown.

My Home

My family's earthen home stands on the peak of a hill, giving a view of my home city. It is a seven-meter-square building with a straw roof. The four walls are painted a traditional gray. THERE IS (a large yard) for the family's leisure time. My father planted a grass lawn, and my mother grows flowers in the garden. The interior of my home has seven rooms. THERE ARE (five bedrooms,) a large combined dining and living room, and a bathroom.

Yenyou Bangole
Gabon

> The horse, the night, and the desert know me,
> the sword, the spear, the paper and pencil, too.
>
> translated by
> *Sami Lazghah*
> Tunisia

Read the following paragraphs. Then do the exercises that follow.

I

My Home

My home is a small cement and brick house in Guayaquil, the biggest city in my country. It _____ located in a nice neighborhood, but there are some old houses around it. My house _____ three bedrooms, a kitchen, two bathrooms, a living room, a dining room, and a service room. There is enough room for my parents, my two brothers, my sisters, and a maid. Outside my house there is a beautiful garden with many flowers. There is also a garage for two cars. Now that I am studying in the United States, and my sister _____ married, my house will seem a little bigger than it really is.

Gustavo Garcia
Ecuador

___ EXERCISE 2D ___

1. Write the correct TO BE and TO HAVE verbs in the blanks.
2. Underline THERE IS and THERE ARE in the paragraph. Circle the subject for each THERE IS/THERE ARE.
3. Why does Gustavo's house seem larger now?
4. What do you remember about Gustavo's house?

II

My Home

In Saudi Arabia, we _____ some restrictions about the
sexes. Men and women _____ separate living areas. Therefore,
we _____ two living rooms, two dining rooms, and several
visitors' rooms. Of course, we also _____ separate bathrooms,
bedrooms, and kitchens. My house _____ two entrances as well,
one for men and the other for women. I live in a very big villa. It is brown
and beige. The villa _____ six bedrooms, five bathrooms, two
kitchens, two living rooms, one drawing room, and one garage.

Adel Salamah
Iran

___ EXERCISE 2E _____

1. Write the correct form of the TO HAVE verbs in each blank.
2. Circle the subject in each sentence.
3. Why does Adel's house have two kitchens and two entrances?
4. Rewrite this paragraph. Use "he," "they," and "his" instead of "I,"
   "we," and "my." Remember to change the verb to agree with its new
   subject:

   I live → he lives

III

_____

Since Hong Kong is well known for its population density,
skyscrapers instead of houses and flats are the most common buildings
that can be found. The building I live in _____ ten floors, and
my apartment _____ on the ninth floor. Two elevators take
people up and down, and each floor _____ eight apartments.
The rooms inside, though small in size, _____ comfortable and

well furnished. There is a sitting room where our family enjoys life. We _____ a television set, a radio, and a tape recorder. After dinner, when everyone has finished his own work, we gather in the sitting room and listen to records or watch television. Since we are no longer children, we do not quarrel with each other, especially when our parents _____ present!

Alice Lo
Hong Kong

—— EXERCISE 2F _____

1. Write the correct form of the TO BE and TO HAVE verbs in each blank.
2. Underline THERE IS. Circle the subject for THERE IS.
3. Write a title for this paragraph.
4. What makes Alice's home different from the other students' homes described in paragraphs I and II?

The Rice Fields

The rice fields are carved in the mountain slope,
fenced in by a row of hills
as far as the eye can see.
The new rice is all dressed in green.
The young maiden in her little hut is weaving
while watching over the rice fields.
Once in a while I hear her chant
a song straight from her heart.

translated by
Irawati Gregory
Indonesia

Write a paragraph about your house. Use some of the questions below to plan your paragraph.

What does your house look like from the outside?

What does the yard around your house look like?

What does your house look like inside?

What things make your house special?

What is your favorite room in your house? Why?

> Although I have to say goodbye,
> I want you to remember me forever, forever.
> Instead of wishing you happiness,
> I'm giving a forget-me-not to you.
>
> translated by
> *Yoko Fukuda*
> Japan

ADVERBS OF FREQUENCY

100% _____	50% _____	0%

<u>always</u>   <u>usually</u>   <u>often</u>   <u>rarely</u>   <u>never</u>

SUBJECT + TO BE + frequency adverb + COMPLEMENT

I   am   <u>always</u>   homesick.

OR

SUBJECT + frequency adverb + TO HAVE + COMPLEMENT

Libya   <u>usually</u>   has   hot weather.

OR

SUBJECT + frequency adverb + OTHER VERBS + COMPLEMENT

She   <u>often</u>   misses   her brother.

NOTE: Placement of adverbs of frequency will vary in some sentences.

What I Miss About My Country

I came to the U.S. only three weeks ago. However, I miss my family very much because I lived with them for twenty years, and I saw them every day. But now I NEVER see them. I also miss Libyan food. I USUALLY cannot find food from my country in the U.S., and I especially miss Libyan coffee. I miss looking at the beach, and I miss the beautiful weather. U.S. weather is different from weather in my country. In Libya the weather is always sunny in the summer, and in the winter it is USUALLY not cold. I miss my friends because I studied with them. We OFTEN took trips together, and they OFTEN visited me. I miss my university too. I miss the library and my teachers. I hope to like the U.S. after I live here a long time.

Mnani-Ely Taiem
Libya

Loneliness

Crow weeps to the dark.
Tide billows in the north wind.
How lonesome the world.

John Shyh-Yuan Wang
China (P.R.C.)

Read the paragraphs below. Then do the exercises that follow.

I

Sadness

I miss many things about my country such as my family, the food, and my friends. Living in the U.S. is difficult because I never have anybody to share my thoughts and experiences. In Venezeula, I used to be with my family every day. Now I am never with them, and it is very hard for me. For example, I often have problems with U.S. food because I am not accustomed to eating hamburgers. I never ate hamburgers before I came to the U.S.A. However, I cannot find typical Venezuelan food in the supermarkets, so I sometimes eat hamburgers. My mother often sends me food from home such as coffee and *arepas*. One more thing I miss about my country is the language. I never hear Spanish. I do not have any friends here because I do not speak English. Therefore, I am always sad now because I miss my country so much.

Evelyn Rios
Venezuela

____ EXERCISE 2G _____

1. Underline 8 adverbs of frequency in the paragraph.
2. Circle the verb that comes before *or* after the adverbs of frequency.
3. Why is Evelyn sad?
4. Why does Evelyn's mother send her Venezuelan food?

II

_____

When my husband decided to come to the U.S., I was very happy because I thought the life in this country might be wonderful. I never studied English before I arrived, and this was my first and biggest difficulty. After a short time, when I realized I was not able to learn quickly, I told my husband, "I want to go back to Italy." Later, I decided to stay with my husband, but I am often sad and homesick. I miss my house, my friends, my relatives, and particularly my nephew. His name is Marco, and he is four years old. When my husband first went to the U.S.A., and I remained in Italy, Marco was angry with him. Marco told me, "Aunt Ginetta, you must look for another husband. I will be your husband!" I don't have any children, and I love Marco like a son. When I write a letter to my family, I always put, "Dear Marco, wait for me. I'm going to return to you soon. I send you my kisses."

Ginetta Longato
Italy

____ EXERCISE 2H _____

1. Put parentheses around 3 adverbs of frequency in the paragraph.
2. Circle the verb that comes before *or* after each adverb of frequency.
3. Write a title for this paragraph.
4. Whom does Ginetta particularly miss?

Why I Miss My Family

My country is one of the smaller countries in Europe, and

it _____ really quiet. I rarely _____ my country
       be   **miss**

because I _____ the U.S.A., but I sometimes _____
        like   **think**

about Swiss cheese, Swiss chocolate, and Swiss fondue! I miss my

family above all. My mother _____ really nice, and I don't
                                be

say that just because she's my mum. She's more than a mother for me.

She's my best friend. Before I left Switzerland, she told me, "Don't worry

about me, and be happy." I also miss my uncle. He _____
                                               be

like a brother to me, and I can always laugh with him. My

grandmother _____ as sweet as her cakes. I love her cakes,
                    be

and I _____ her, too. She always _____ about
        love   **think**

other people and never about herself. I miss her. Finally, I miss my cat

Zorro. Do you think it's crazy to miss a cat? Perhaps. But I can't change

my mind. I miss Zorro. My family isn't a special family, but it's my own

family, and I miss everyone!

Annick Burkhalter
Switzerland

_____ EXERCISE 21 _____

1. Write the correct form of the present tense verbs in the blanks.
2. Circle the subject for each of the verbs in the blanks.
3. Put parentheses around 5 frequency adverbs.
4. What is amusing about this paragraph?

IV

East or West, Home Is Best

I miss my country so much. Every day I think about the sea and the sun. In my country, I always _____ to the sea to play and
go

relax. I _____ the whole summer in the sun. But in the United
spend

States, there is no beach, and I never have time to relax. I also miss my home and my family. I _____ the evenings we spent together,
miss

watching TV and drinking tea. I miss these things because here I do not have a close friend, and I do not have a family. Here we _____
have

dinner at five o'clock. In Libya, we usually have dinner at one o'clock, so the family _____ tea at five o'clock. Everything _____
have   *be*

different here, even the time of dinner. Finally, I miss my university so much, and I miss my friends there. Every Friday, my friends and I always had a small party. I miss that party a lot. I miss everything about my country.

Nurelhuda Ali Bassuine
Libya

___ EXERCISE 2J _____

1. Write the correct present tense verbs in the blanks.
2. Put parentheses around 4 adverbs of frequency.
   Circle the verbs that come before *or* after the frequency adverbs.
3. Underline THERE IS. Put brackets [   ] around the subject of THERE IS.
4. What advice would you give to Nurelhuda to help her be happier?

Migratory Bird

Bird, are you leaving? Fly me to your home with you on your feathered back.

translated by
T. Kim
Korea

INTERVIEW

Ask a classmate the questions below. Write the answers to the questions. Use adverbs of frequency in your sentences.

What do you always miss about your hometown?

What do you usually miss about your hometown?

What do you often miss about your hometown?

What do you sometimes miss about your hometown?

What do you rarely miss about your hometown?

What do you never miss about your hometown?

What do you have to do every day? (Always)

What do you usually have to do?

What do you often have to do?

What do you sometimes have to do?

What do you rarely have to do?

What do you never have to do?

Now, rewrite your paragraph. Change the he/she, his/hers, *and* him/her *to* I, me, *and* my. *Be sure that the verbs you use agree with the subjects.*

Why can't I wave it away?
Why can't I erase it?
I miss my hometown, and
I feel sad to recall the people there
A thousand million miles away,
When will we be able to get together?

translated by
Chia-Chon Pin
Taiwan (R.O.C.)

Write a paragraph about what you miss about your country (or about something else you miss). Answer some of the questions below.

What do you miss? Why?
Who do you miss? Why?
What do you always miss? Why?
Who do you always miss? Why?

Now make a list of ideas for your paragaph.

WHAT I MISS ABOUT MY COUNTRY

What?	*Why?*
food	because _____
house	because _____
school	because _____
?????	because _____

Who?	*Why?*
brother	because _____
friend	because _____
teacher	because _____
?????	because _____

Come from far away, stay with me.
You're my glorious sun.
You must stay, don't ask me why.
Stay and destroy all the ice.
Don't ask me why.
Be with me all the time.

                    translated by
                    Reza Mohseni Motlagh
                    Iran

NEGATIVE *TO BE* AND *TO HAVE* VERBS

TO BE

Present		Past	
I	am <u>not</u>	I	was <u>not</u>
he she it	is <u>not</u>	he she it	was <u>not</u>
you we they	are <u>not</u>	you we they	were <u>not</u>

TO HAVE

Present		Past	
I	<u>do not</u> have	I	<u>did not</u> have
he she it	<u>does not</u> have	he she it	<u>did not</u> have
you we they	<u>do not</u> have	you we they	<u>did not</u> have

---

The Seasons in My Country

Colombia has two seasons, winter and summer. It <u>DOES NOT HAVE</u> spring or autumn. In the winter, it rains frequently. People prefer to stay in their houses because the temperature is cool, but it <u>IS NOT</u> cold. The trees and the flowers grow, so you can see many colors: green, yellow, and red. Also you can smell delicious aromas. Everybody wears coats, scarves, and sweaters, and they drink hot coffee. In the summer, we <u>DO NOT HAVE</u> rain. The sun shines all day long. People like to go to parks and travel to other cities. The temperature is hot. For this reason, everybody wears light clothes. The trees and flowers grow, but they <u>ARE NOT</u> as fresh. I like summer because I can go to my farm with my family.

Maria Muñoz
Colombia

Read the paragraphs on page 47. Then do the exercises that follow.

I

The Seasons

Winter and summer are the seasons in Caracas, Venezuela. We do not have fall and spring. I prefer the winter because it is not too hot. In the winters, it rains a lot of the time. During the day, we have warmth, but we are not hot. On winter evenings we are cool. There are smells of the rivers and smells of the wet earth. The people in my hometown prefer winter because it is prettier. There are many flowers, and the green of the trees is very beautiful. The birds are very colorful, and they sing in the trees. The rain swells the rivers, and the rivers become brown. There are fresh fruits all the time.

Natalia Guerra
Venezuela

—— EXERCISE 2K ————————————————————

1. Underline the negative TO HAVE and TO BE verbs in the paragraph.
2. Circle the subjects in the negative TO HAVE and TO BE sentences.
3. Put parentheses around the THERE IS and THERE ARE sentences. Circle the subject in those sentences.
4. Why does Natalia prefer the winter in Venezuela?

II

The Seasons in My Hometown

Riyadh, the capital of Saudi Arabia, has four seasons. But the seasons are not the same length. Summer is four months long, and it is very hot. The schools are closed, and some people go to the sea to swim. Many people go to Taif City because it is not so hot in the mountains. I like the summer because it is not cold. At noon the air is very hot because the sun is shining. The spring and fall seasons in my country are only two months long. During these seasons, the air is very comfortable, and the trees are green. Some people travel to Medina because they want to visit the mosque. Other people travel outside the country because they do not have to work. The winter in Saudi Arabia is four months long. The weather is very cold. There is a lot of rain. Sometimes the weather is nice, but often it is not.

Hassan Hareeri
Saudi Arabia

1. Circle the negative TO HAVE and TO BE verbs in the paragraph.
2. Put parentheses around the subjects in the underlined sentences.
3. Which season does Hassan prefer? Why?
4. How many times does Hassan use the words *weather* and *seasons* in the paragraph? Why?

> I long for autumn,
> for the blue sky and drifting clouds.
> Join me, oh! you yellow butterfly.
> We'll sing and dance over that fragrant rose.
>
> *Van Tran*
> Vietnam

NEGATIVE REGULAR VERBS

Present		Past		
I	do not like*	I	did not	talk*
he she it	does not come*	he she it	did not	go* feel* see*
you we they	do not walk*	you we they	did not	live* take* drink*

NOTE: The root form of the verb is used with the negative.

Read the paragraphs below. Then do the exercises that follow.

I

The Seasons in Somalia

In my city, and in my country, we have four seasons: summer, fall, winter, and spring. In the summer, every place is green, and the weather is warm and sunny. <u>Then eveyone can be comfortable and happy.</u> Most people in Somalia like the summer because they do not feel cold, and they do not wear sweaters. In the fall, there is not any rain, and the weather is cold. <u>The leaves fall from the trees.</u> There is not any rain in the winter, either, but the weather is very hot. Finally, in the spring there is a lot of rain. <u>It is a season of great activity.</u> The farmers grow crops on their farms, and there is plenty of grass for the animals.

Mohamed Isse
Somalia

___ EXERCISE 2M _____

1. Underline the negative verbs (TO HAVE, TO BE, and PRESENT TENSE regular verbs) in the paragraph.

2. Put parentheses around the THERE IS and THERE ARE in the paragraph.

3. Make the underlined sentences negative.

4. How many times does Mohamed use the words *seasons* and *weather* in the paragraph? Why?

II

The Many Seasons in Turkey

If you go to Turkey, you can see three seasons at the same time. If you go to eastern Turkey, you will see that the weather is very cold. It is dark because the sun does not shine. There are not any leaves, and the roads are icy. People ski, but a lot of people also get sick because of the cold weather. <u>Snow covers the entire area,</u> and the people are not happy. But if you go to western Turkey, you will see spring. There are flowers, green grass, fruit, and sunshine. Western Turkey is a very good area. <u>A lot of people live there.</u> You will also see a lot of tourists. If you go to South Turkey, you will see the summer season. There is sunlight, and you will see flowers, fruits, green grass, and the sea. <u>A lot of men take sun baths because the sea is very cool.</u> There are many crops and products like fruits and vegetables for sale.

Mustafa Aytac
Turkey

___ EXERCISE 2N _____

1. Underline all the negative verbs in the paragraph.

2. Underline THERE IS and THERE ARE. Circle the subjects in those sentences.

3. Make the underlined sentences negative.

4. Would you go to eastern Turkey for a vacation?

In drowsy spring, I
saw a cow standing in a
field of drizzling rain.

translated by
Mari Kanada
Japan

___ WRITING ASSIGNMENT ___

*Write a paragraph about the seasons in your hometown. Use the
chart below to help plan your paragraph. Answer some of the
questions below.*

How many seasons do you have in your hometown?

What do you remember about each season?

Which season is your favorite season?

Why?

Which season do you dislike?

Why?

SEASONS

Adjectives	What do you see? hear? smell?
hot	
warm	
cold	
cool	
humid	
dry	
rainy	
windy	
snow	
ice	
green	

Ask a person NOT in your class to describe the seasons in his or her hometown. Ask some of the questions from the writing assignment above. Then write the answers in a paragraph. Use correct subject pronouns. Make sure each verb agrees with its subject. Use the chart below to indicate the differences in temperature between Fahrenheit and centigrade. Use sentences like:

In the winter, the temperature ranges from _____ degrees C. (_____ degrees Fahrenheit) to _____ degrees C.

In the summer, the temperature reaches _____ degrees C. (_____ degrees F.).

TEMPERATURE CONVERSION

C° -40 -20 0 20 40 60 80 100 120 140 160 180 200 220 240 260

F° -40 -20 0 20 40 60 80 100 120 140 160 180 200 220 240 260 280 300 320 340 360 380 400 420 440 460 480 500

Study the information in the box below. Then do the exercises and the writing assignment that follow.

HAIKU

Haiku: a Japanese poem about nature that has 17 syllables.

line 1 = 5 syllables
line 2 = 7 syllables
line 3 = 5 syllables

Winter

1   2 3 4 5   (5 syllables)
Warmth, already gone.

1 2 3 4 5 6 7   (7 syllables)
The cold has entered the town.

1 2   3 4 5   (5 syllables)
Put your sweater on!

Said Pirnazar
Iran

Read the haiku written by students below. Count the syllables.
Some of the haiku are not exactly correct.

Spring

Spring breeze comes to wake   _____ syllables

trees up, to begin new life   _____ syllables

after winter's sleep.   _____ syllables

Aziz Goharani
Iran

Summer

Nice smelling weather   _____ syllables

bright flowers bloom everywhere   _____ syllables

waiting for their end.   _____ syllables

Ziya Bozer
Turkey

Autumn

Sounds of ruffling leaves   _____ syllables

and the crispy air we breathe   _____ syllables

is the autumn breeze.   _____ syllables

Boyle Gaffar
Indonesia

Winter

Little pussy cat   _____ syllables

crouched in the dark corner: _____ syllables

a soft woolen ball.   _____ syllables

Wai Ming Li
Hong Kong

Snow

It came from the sky   _____ syllables

like falling gleaming stars   _____ syllables

dressing the earth in white.   _____ syllables

Jose Viani
Venezuela

Evening

Far out in the west   _____ syllables

as the big red bulb drops,   _____ syllables

the silent world rests.   _____ syllables

Wai Ming Li
Hong Kong

___ WRITING ASSIGNMENT _____

Think about the seasons in your country. Then write a haiku about one of the seasons. Count the syllables. Try to follow the correct form of the poem.

OTHER PARAGRAPH TOPICS

My Present Hometown

My Favorite Room in My Present Home

How I Feel When It Rains (or Snows)

The Seasons in Another Part of My Country

The Seasons in My Present Hometown

WRITING PROJECTS

Individual Booklets

Use the paragraph(s) you have written to begin a booklet about your hometown and about your home. Then write several more paragraphs about your hometown and your home. Illustrate the booklet with drawings and/or photographs. Use some of the titles below:

My Friend's House

My School

Shops in My Hometown

My Favorite Place in My Hometown

A Park in My Hometown

The Most Beautiful Building in My Hometown

My Favorite Season in My Hometown

Use photographs of your hometown and your home to make your booklet more interesting. Make a colorful cover for your booklet. Display the booklet in your classroom, and invite other students from other classes to your classroom to see the booklets.

Group Project

Each student should write several haiku. Gather the haiku into a booklet. Decorate the pages and the cover of the booklet with small drawings and/or photographs of nature and the seasons. Make copies of the booklet for all the members of the class.

Three

Country I

My Country's Flag

The Colombian flag's colors are yellow, blue, and red. These three colors are placed in horizontal bars, and the yellow stripe is double the size of the blue and red stripes. That is, the yellow bar is equal to both the red and the blue bars. The color yellow means the wealth of our soil; the gold mineral represents this wealth, and the yellow stripe is placed at the top of the flag. The middle bar is blue. It means the two oceans, the Atlantic and the Pacific, that border our territory. The last color, red, means the blood that was lost by our patriots to obtain liberty from Spain. This flag is similar to the flags of Eucador and Venezuela because originally these three countries were united under the name of Gran Colombia (Great Colombia).

Danilo Valencia
Colombia

PREPOSITIONS OF PLACE

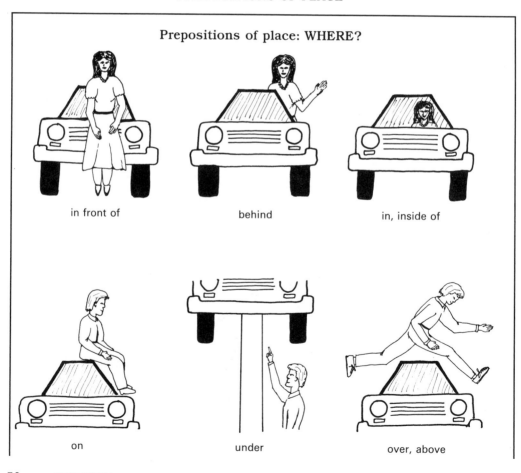

Prepositions of place: WHERE?

in front of

behind

in, inside of

on

under

over, above

beside   between

PREPOSITIONAL PHRASES

PHRASE: a group of words that does <u>NOT</u> have a subject and/or does <u>NOT</u> have a verb.

Prepositional Phrase:

PREPOSITION + ARTICLE (a, an, the) + (adjective) + NOUN

Sample Prepositional Phrases of Place

The stars are (*in* **the corner**).

The stripes are (*on* **the white part**).

The eagle appears (*beside* **the circle**).

The moon is (*under* **the stripe**).

The star is (*between* **the red stripe and the white stripe**).

The five points (*on* **the star**) represent five countries.

The triangle is (*beside* **the circle**).

The moon is (*above* **the stars**).

Other Important Prepositions

The red color represents the blood (*of* **the people**).

Blue represents peace (*with* **all the people**) (*of* **the world**).

Our flag was designed (*by* **the patriots**) (*in* **our country**).

Green stands (*for* **the prosperity**) (*in* **our country**).

We carry our flag (*to* **our school**).

Indonesia's Flag

We Indonesians call our flag Merah-Pusih. *Merah* means "red," and *pusih* means "white." Our flag is rectangular. The width is two-thirds (*of the length*). It consists (*of two equal parts*), divided horizontally (*in the middle*). The color (*of the top part*) is red, and the bottom part is white. Red represents courage, and white means peace. Historically, the meaning (*of the flag*) is that Indonesians are brave. They also seek peace among themselves and (*with other countries*) (*in the world*). (*On a special day*), like Independence Day (**August 17**), we raise the flag (*on a pole*)(*in front*)(*of each house*). We love and admire our flag very much. (*On **Independence Day***), the flag is raised while the independence song is played (*by a band*). Usually the military bands play that song very well, so my love and pride (*of my country*) is aroused.

Istimawan Dipohusodo
Indonesia

Read the paragraphs below. Then do the exercises that follow.

I

The Flag of Somalia

Our country's flag looks like the sky. It is blue, and it has a white star with five points in the middle of the flag. <u>The five-pointed star stands for the five parts of Somalia.</u> Our flag was created by the freedom pioneers in my country in October 1954. Before that time, Somalia was an Italian and an English colony.

Abdinazak Mohamed Osman
Somalia

1. Put 8 prepositional phrases in parentheses.
2. Circle the noun (or pronoun) that follows each preposition.
3. What question could you ask Abdinazak about the underlined sentence?
4. Draw a picture of Somalia's flag.

II

My Country's Flag

Every country has its own flag. Each flag _____ different colors and shapes which have different meanings. The flag of Vietnam does not look like any flag from any other country. My country's flag _____ simple. It _____ a yellow rectangle. There _____ three horizontal red stripes which go across from one end to the other end of the flag. The yellow color represents the color of my countrymen's skin. The three red lines represent three different areas in my country. These areas _____ North, Central, and South Vietnam. The red color represents the blood of my country. An overall meaning of my country's flag _____ that people with yellow skin live in three different areas which combine together as a country that _____ called Vietnam.

Minh Chu
Vietnam

_____ EXERCISE 3B _____

1. Write the correct form of the verb TO BE and the verb TO HAVE in each blank.
2. Put parentheses around 10 prepositional phrases.
3. Circle the noun (or pronoun) in each prepositional phrase.
4. What do you remember about the Vietnamese flag?

___ **INTERVIEW**

*Ask a friend <u>not</u> from your country to describe his or her coun-
try's flag. As your friend describes the flag, draw the flag. Then
show your friend your drawing. Is it correct? What information
did your friend need to tell you?*

CLAUSES

CLAUSE: a group of words with a subject (**S**) and a verb (**V**), and perhaps a complement (**C**).

$$\quad\quad\quad S \quad\quad\quad V \quad\quad\quad C \quad\quad\quad S$$
<u>My country's flag</u> (is) (a rectangle). <u>Its color</u>

$$V \quad C \quad S \quad V \quad\quad\quad C$$
(is) (red). <u>It</u> (has) (a green star in the middle).

---

*Read the paragraph below. <u>Underline</u> the subject of each clause
(S). (Circle) the verb in each clause (V). Put parentheses ( )
around the complement (C).*

My Country's Flag

My country's flag is a rectangle. The color is red. It has a green star in
the middle. The red part of the flag stands for blood. The people of Morocco
fought hard for independence. A lot of blood was spread all over the country.
The green star in the middle of the flag stands for peace and prosperity. Mo-

rocco gained independence from France in 1956. The people started to work hard to improve the social and economic situation. I am proud of my country's flag. I know the meaning of independence.

Abdelkader Assal
Morocco

JOINING TWO CLAUSES

TO JOIN TWO CLAUSES: S + V (+ C) ⎣, and⎦ S + V (+ C).

Its color (is) red ⎣, and⎦ it (has) a green star in the middle. The red part of the flag (stands) for blood. The people of Morocco (fought) hard for independence ⎣, and⎦ a lot of blood (was spread) all over the country. The green star in the middle of my country's flag (stands) for peace and prosperity. Morocco (gained) independence from France in 1956 ⎣, and⎦ the people (started) to work hard to improve the social and economic situations. I (am) proud of my country's flag ⎣, and⎦ I (know) the meaning of independence.

Abdelkader Assal
Morocco

____ EXERCISE 3C _____

Read the paragraph on page 62. Underline the subject of each clause. Circle the verb in each clause. Put a box around the ⎣, and⎦ *that joins two clauses.*

Sri Lanka's National Flag

My country's flag is very beautiful. The background of the flag is yellow , and there is a picture of a lion with a sword on the flag. The people of my country have a relationship with the lion , and therefore special courage is with us. There are also two stripes of orange and green on our flag , and there are four *bo* leaves in the four corners. The four *bo* leaves are related to our religion , and they stand for peace and loving kindness. Most of the Sri Lankan people are Buddhists , and we respect the *bo* tree as a sacred tree. Our religious leader, the Lord Buddha, was enlightened under a *bo* tree.

B. D. Pathinyake
Sri Lanka

___ EXERCISE 3D _____

Read the paragraphs below. Underline the subject of each clause. Circle the verb in each clause. Put a box around [. and] *that joins two clauses.*

I

The Flag of the People's Republic of China

The flag of the People's Republic of China (P.R.C.) is called the "Five Stars Red Flag." The flag is oblong , and its color is red. There are five yellow stars in the upper left corner of the flag. One of the stars is large , and the others are small. The large star is in the center , and the others surround it. The red stands for socialism in the P.R.C. , and the yellow stars mean that the Chinese are a yellow people. The biggest star stands for the Communist party. The four smaller stars represent all the people in China. The red color also has another meaning. It stands for the blood of the great number of Chinese heroes. The founding of the P.R.C. is the result of innumerable people who died for their country.

Dong Aichu
China (P.R.C.)

II

The Flag of Malaysia

Malaysia's flag looks like the U.S. flag. It has thirteen red and white horizontal stripes. The first stripe is red , and the second is white. This pattern continues until the thirteenth is red. A square of blue is in the upper left corner of the flag , and a yellow half-moon with one big star beside it is on the blue square. The thirteen stripes on the flag stand for the thirteen states in Malaysia. The red stripes represent the courage of the Malaysians　, and　the white stripes stand for the honesty of Malaysians. Malaysia is an Islamic country. Therefore, the moon and the star are the symbols of Islam as the first religion in Malaysia.

Nazari Mohamed
Malaysia

Drum

You beat a message,
Its joyful tempo a pledge:
Birth, wedding. A woe
its hoarse note:
Death, sorrow, foe.
Drum, breath of ancestors.

translated by
Yenyou Bangole
Gabon

INTERVIEW

Ask a friend NOT in your class and NOT from your country to describe his or her country's flag. Then, with your friend's help, draw a picture of that flag. Finally, write a paragraph describing the flag. Ask your friend any questions that are necessary to complete the paragraph.
During the class, exchange paragraphs with a classmate.

A. Read the paragraph.

B. Draw a picture of the flag described in the paragraph.

C. Compare your picture with the picture your classmate drew. Was some information about the flag missing from the paragraph?

My country, you have my heart and my love.
My country, you must stay free,
And I depend on my God.

translated by
Tarik A. Tawfic
Egypt

Read the paragraphs below. Then do the exercises that follow.

I

The Flag of Korea

If you want to learn about Korean philosophy, you should study our flag. It holds the essence of orientalism. Because our flag is complex, I will draw a picture of the flag. First, the background of the flag is white. This color stands for the peace and the innocence of the Korean people. Three black lines, some broken and some unbroken, are drawn diagonally at the four corners of the flag, and they represent the four seasons. The meaning of the three broken lines is spring. Four lines represent summer, five lines is fall, and six lines is winter. The continuous black lines are positive, and the broken lines are negative. A circle placed at the center of the flag represents the balance of space and nature. The circle is divided into two parts, and we call this curved line the *taeguk* mark. The upper half is red, and it signifies positive, light, man, and heaven. The lower half is blue, and it signifies negative, dark, woman, and the earth. Together, the positive and negative aspects of our flag signify the Korean people's love of balance and harmony.

Yong Ha Park
Korea

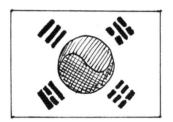

___ EXERCISE 3E _____

1. Put parentheses around 12 prepositional phrases.
2. Underline the noun (or pronoun) that follows each preposition.
3. Draw boxes around ⌊, and⌋ joining the two clauses.
4. Make the underlined clauses negative.

II

The Flag of Taiwan, the Republic of China

There are three different colors in our country's flag: red, blue, and white. It was designed by one of the national heroes of our country, H. T. Lu, seventy-three years ago. On the surface of our country's flag, the white star in the upper right corner _____ like the sun is just
look

hanging in the center of the sky. The blue color _____ the
represent

blue sky around all of us, and the red color _____ for blood
stand

which was shed when the revolution succeeded. In the left corner of my country's flag, the white circle and twelve angles _____
mean

the sun is shining and hanging above our heads. Around this "sun,"

the blue color _____ the sky is very beautiful and there
mean

_____ not any clouds in it. The rest of the flag, with its
be

red color, means that the world is full of hope and happiness.

Wei-Fuu Yang
Taiwan (R.O.C.)

___ EXERCISE 3F _____

1. Write the correct present tense verbs in the blanks.
2. Put parentheses around 20 prepositional phrases.
3. Draw the Taiwanese flag.
4. What additional information do you need to draw the flag? What questions should you ask the author to complete your drawing?

_____ EXERCISE 3G _____

*Read the paragraph below. It has many short clauses. Join
some of the clauses with* [, and] . *An asterisk (*) indicates
where you should join the clauses. Do NOT capitalize the first
word of the second clause.*

The National Flag of Brazil

*and e*Brazil's flag is composed of four colors. It has four geometric figures*x,*
* Each one of them represents something important about Brazil's people
or Brazil's history. Together they form a beautful and harmonious combina-
tion. The flag is a green rectangle. * It represents Brazilian forests. Brazil
is located mainly in the Amazonian region. * It is tropical and very green.
There is a bright yellow stripe across the flag. * The yellow stands for the
gold mined in Brazil. In the center of the flag, above the stripe, is a blue
circle with stars. Blue is the color of Brazil's sky. * The white stars in the
circle are a famous constellation. In the circle is the phrase, "Order and
Progress." This motto encourages the Brazilian people to improve their way
of life.

José Nilson Campos
Brazil

_____ WRITING ASSIGNMENT _____

*Draw a picture of your country's flag. Then write a paragraph
about your country's flag. Answer some of the questions below.*

What colors are on the flag?

What do those colors mean?

What shapes are on the flag?

What does each shape mean?

Where is each color, and each shape, located on the flag?

Exchange paragraphs with a classmate.

    A. Read your classmate's paragraph.

    B. Draw the flag your classmate describes in that paragraph.

    C. Ask your classmate any questions that are necessary to complete the picture of the flag.

    D. Answer any questions your classmate asks about your country's flag.

Each wrong step is a lost destiny, and each problem in life is a gained experience.

translated by
Semoa de Sousa
Sao Tomé, West Africa

MORE PREPOSITIONS

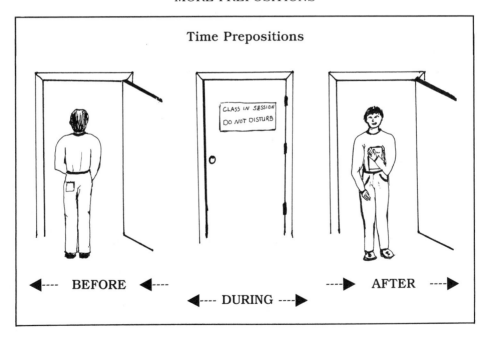

Time Prepositions

CLASS IN SESSION
DO NOT DISTURB

◀--- **BEFORE** ◀----   ---▶ **AFTER** ---▶

                    ◀--- **DURING** ---▶

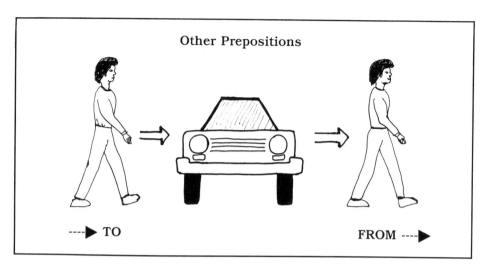

Other Prepositions

----▶ TO   FROM ----▶

SAMPLE PREPOSITIONAL PHRASES

El Salvador was a Spanish colony (*before* **our independence**).

OR

(*Before* **our independence**), El Salvador was a Spanish colony.

We went home (*after* **the party**).

OR

(*After* **the party**), we went home.

Luis wore a costume (*during* **the celebration**).

OR

(*During* **the celebration**), Luis wore a costume.

The soldiers marched (*from* **the Capitol**) (*to* **the White House**).

The students (*from* **Indonesia**) came (*to* **the celebration**).

Indonesia's Celebration

Every year, (*on* **August 17th**), all Indonesians celebrate Independence Day. Indonesia gained independence (*on* **August 17, 1945**) (*after* **the Second World War**). (*After* **the war**), Indonesia began to develop the economics (*of* **the country**) and to educate its people. Although I am now (*in* **the United States**), I still celebrate my country's Independence Day. This year I invited my Indonesian friends and some American friends to come (*to* **my house**) (*for* **a party**). I prepared Indonesian food, and we celebrated all day.

Wishnoe Saleh Thaib
Indonesia

Read the paragraphs below. Then do the exercises that follow.

I

A Holiday in Iraq

In Iraq, my native country, we have the celebration of a historical event. It is called the Nawros Feast. It is on March 21st every year. People all over Iraq celebrate this event. They go to parks, mountains, and gardens. They spend a nice day. This event expresses freedom from the tyranny that existed in Kurdish history two thousand years ago. At that time, there was a man called "Kawo." He killed the ruler who was unfair. The ruler caused many bad things to happen to the people, and he harmed many people. Now, people celebrate his death, and they remember the tyranny. Every year, people show their happiness, and they look forward to the future with hope.

Amin Diyar
Iraq

_____ EXERCISE 3H _____

1. Put parentheses around 8 prepositional phrases. Circle the noun (or pronoun) that follows each preposition.
2. Identify the subject (S) and the verb (V) in each underlined sentence.
3. Put a box around each [. and] that joins two clauses in this paragraph. Identify the subject (S) and the verb (V) in each of the clauses.
4. How do people in Iraq celebrate Independence Day?

II

Carnival in Brazil

There is a big party in Brazil which is called "Carnival." It usually occurs during the last part of February. For three days, people listen to the traditional music that is called *samba*, and everybody _____

have

a good time. During the carnival, people _____ happy. * Some

be

of them wear funny dresses and _____ their faces with many

paint

colors. On the second day, there _____ a beautiful parade on the

be

principal street of each city. People _____ costumes. * They

wear

dance. They throw candies to the other people. * They _____

throw

confetti, too. On the last day, there _____ another beautiful

be

parade. People _____ into the streets. They watch the "escola de

go

samba." In this beautiful dance, the people wear colorful costumes. After the "escola de samba," there _____ many parties. * People go

be

to the parties in their costumes. In some cases, the men _____

dress

like women, or they put masks on their faces. In conclusion, during the carnival party, everybody _____ a wonderful time.

have

Ademir Castro
Brazil

—— EXERCISE 31 ——————————————————————

1. Write the correct present tense verbs in the blanks.
2. Put parentheses around 16 prepositional phrases. Circle the noun (or pronoun) that follows each preposition.
3. Underline the subject that follows each THERE IS or THERE ARE.
4. Join two clauses with ⌐, and⌐ where you see the asterisks (*).

SUBJECT-VERB AGREEMENT

Singular		*Plural*
Somebody	IS	
Everybody	HAS	ARE
Nobody	COOKS	HAVE
Something	HAPPENS	People { WALK
Everything	GOES	GO
Someone	WALKS	LISTEN
Everyone	LISTENS	

Read the paragraphs below. Then do the exercises that follow.

I

The Most Famous Holiday in My Country

One holiday in my country is Eid Aladha Almubarak. The reason for the holiday is to remember the time when the prophet Ibraham needed to kill his son Ishmail after his dream. Ibraham knew that his dream was from God because every prophet who dreamed anything about a person he loved very much knew the dream was an order from God. The morning after his dream, Ibraham told his son. * His son accepted it. When Ibraham began to kill his son, God sent a sheep to Ibraham to kill. The sheep was called "Adhia." Then Ibraham did not kill his son. From that day, most Muslims kill a sheep on the feast of Eid Aladha. On this day, the Muslims visit each other. * They cook a delicious meal with special food. The people give the children money to celebrate this day. * All of them are happy on this day.

Ameen Alawi
United Arab Emirates

1. Put parentheses around 8 prepositional phrases. Circle the noun (or the pronoun) that follows each preposition.
2. Identify the subject (S) and the verb (V) in each underlined sentence.
3. Join two clauses with ⌐, and⌐ where you see an asterisk.
4. What questions could you ask Ameen about this holiday?

II

Independence Day

One of the biggest holidays in Cape Verde is Independence Day, on July 5. This day symbolizes freedom from colonial domination, exploitation, and slavery. The people endured colonialism for many years. * They struggled hard for a better education for their children. In other words, they were struggling to improve their situation. On Independence Day, the President gives a long speech. He talks about the founder of the political group who was killed. * He talks about himself when he was a prisoner. He announces the progress of the country. * He gives the plans that the government has for the future. The speech of the President is followed by a wonderful military parade. Also, there is a big popular party with the best musical group. Some people dance. The marchers exhibit the pictures of the people who died in the struggle for national liberation. When the Cape Verdian people became independent, they felt that they were really free and able to realize their dreams. Therefore, they enjoy this holiday every year.

Isaurinda Baptista
Cape Verde, West Africa

1. What is the main idea in this paragraph?
2. Identify the subject (S) and the (V) in each underlined sentence.
3. Join two clauses with ⌐, and⌐ where you see the asterisks.
4. How do people in Cape Verde celebrate Independence Day?

—— **WRITING ASSIGNMENT** ——

1. Write a paragraph about a famous holiday in your country. Answer some of the questions below.

What is the name of the holiday?

Is it a religious holiday?

Is it a political holiday?

When is it?

How do people celebrate the holiday?

What is special about the celebration?

    Do the people wear costumes?

    Do they eat special foods?

    Do they have special parties?

What traditions are celebrated?

What customs are celebrated?

2. *Exchange paragraphs with a classmate.*

  A. Read the paragraph.

  B. Ask your classmate any questions you have about the holiday.

  C. Put parentheses around the prepositional phrases in your classmate's paragraph.

  D. Draw a box around each | , and | that joins two clauses.

> If you love something,
> leave it free.
> If it comes back to you, it's yours.
> But if it does not come back,
> it never was yours.
>
> translated by
> *Lorena Gabrie*
> Honduras

Read the paragraphs below. Then do the exercises that follow.

I

Chinese New Year

Chinese New Year is a public holiday in my home country, Malaysia. I usually look forward to this day so that I can have a lot of fun like getting red-packets from my elders and watching the lion dance. The

red-packet _____ a traditional Chinese gift from the elders
                 be

to the young generations when they greet them on New Year's Day.

Everybody _____ happy to receive the red-packet because
                    be

it _____ good luck and a good start at the beginning of the new
     represent

year. Inside the red-packet there is money. There is no specific sum. It

can be fifty cents or five dollars or ten dollars. Nobody _____

                                                                      care

about the amount. Lion dancing _____ another Chinese tradition
                                          be

for the new year. It _____ several people. First, there are two
                          need

people covered with the lion costume, and there are others who play a big

drum, cymbals, and other instruments. The "lion" _____ down
                                                              dance

the street, and it _____ good luck. Therefore, a lot of people
                        mean

_____ the lion back to their homes. When the lion _____
     invite   **come**

to a house, the family _____ a red-packet to a stick and raises
                             tie

the stick high in the air. The lion _____ the stick to get the
                                          climb

red-packet.

Man-Chiu Lu
Malaysia

—— EXERCISE 3L _____

1. Write the correct present tense verbs in the blanks.
2. Underline THERE IS/THERE ARE in the paragraph. Circle the subject that follows each THERE IS or THERE ARE.
3. Underline "everybody," "nobody," and "people" in the paragraph.
   Put brackets [ ] around the verb that follows each.
4. Write two questions that you could ask Man-Chiu that would help
   you know more about Chinese New Year.

II

Celebrating the Japanese Rice Harvest

My favorite holiday _____ on the first Sunday of October. On
          be

that day, we _____ the rice harvest. We _____ a big
          celebrate   **have**

festival at our local shrine on this holy day. There _____ many
                                                    be

booths along the path to the shrine. People _____ food such as
                                          buy

crepes, ice cream, cookies, and cakes. My favorite cake _____
                                                      be

waffle sweet. It _____ like a soft cloud shining in the sunset. In
          look

the early morning, my mother and sister _____ a special dinner.
                                      prepare

They _____ to great efforts in the kitchen. Generally *sushi*
     go

_____ the main dish. When all my relatives _____
be   **come**

together, my home _____ festive. My nieces and nephews
                become

_____ and _____ around. Because I _____ to
sing   **dance**   **like**

see children making happy noise, I do not mind at all. I _____
                                                      have

a very good time on this special day.

Mitsuaki Uchida
Japan

___ EXERCISE 3M ___

1. Write the correct present tense verbs in the blanks. Circle the subject for each of those verbs.
2. What is the main idea of this paragraph?
3. Put parentheses around 10 prepositional phrases. Circle the noun (or the pronoun) that follows each preposition.
4. Rewrite this paragraph. Change "I," "we," and "my" to "she," "they," and "her." Be sure that each verb agrees with its subject.

III

Hajj

Hajj _____ the most popular holiday in my country. It
      be

is an Islamic holiday, and it is in the last month of the year. People

_____ from far away to Medina and Mecca to visit these holy
   come

cities. Some people do not go to the holy cities because they do not have

money or they are not well. The Quran says that these people can

_____ to Mecca or Medina another year. At least one time
  go

during their lives, they must go to Mecca. People who do not travel to

holy cities fast on the feast of Hajj. On the second day, Muslims

_____ together with friends. They cook meat, and the children
  gather

wear new clothes.

Faizah Ahmad
Saudi Arabia

—— EXERCISE 3N ——————————————————

1. Write the correct present tense verbs in the blanks.
2. Underline the negative verbs in this paragraph.
3. Make the underlined sentences negative.
4. Write two questions that you could ask Faizah about Hajj.

If someone wants to live,
he will have to surmount every difficulty.
History shows that
all people who do not work seriously
have great problems in surviving.

translated by
Fakhreddine Karray
Tunisia

____ INTERVIEW _____

Interview a friend NOT in your class and NOT from your country about a holiday in his/her country. Ask some of the questions on pages 72 and 73. Then write the paragraph.

Exchange paragraphs with a classmate.

    A. Read the paragraph.

    B. Put the prepositional phrases in parentheses.

    C. Draw a box around two clauses joined with ⌐, and⌐ .

OTHER WRITING ASSIGMENTS

    My Favorite Vacation Place in My Country

    My Favorite Book

    My Favorite Sport

    What I Do on a Weekday in My Country

    What I Do on a Weekend Day in My Country

WRITING PROJECTS

Individual Project

    Write several paragraphs about several different holidays in your country. Write paragraphs about some of the topics below.

    My Favorite Holiday

    Traditional Dress for Women During _____ Holiday

    Traditional Dress for Men During _____ Holiday

    A Famous Person Who Is Honored by a Holiday in My Country

    Preparing for _____ Holiday in My Country

    A Special Holiday in My Hometown

Make a booklet with the paragraphs about famous holidays in your country. Include in the booklet photographs or drawings of traditional dress and costume of those celebrations. Decorate the booklet with drawings or photographs of the celebrations. Give the booklet to a public school library to use with the students in that school.

Group Project

Make a booklet of flags of many countries of the world. Gather colorful pictures of flags of the countries of the students in class. You may include flags of other countries as well. Write paragraphs that describe the meanings of the flags. Present the booklet to a public school library to use with the students in that school.

Four

Country II

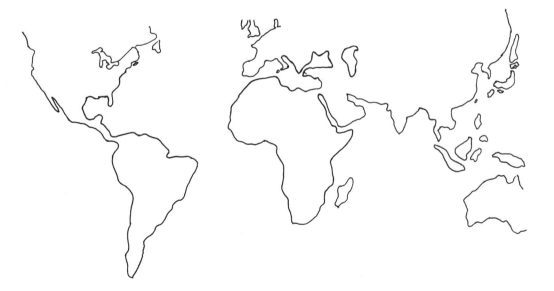

Fathers and Mothers

A proverb in China says, "Fathers are outdoors, mothers are indoors." It means that fathers have to work hard for the support of the family, so they have to be outdoors—to work. And mothers are considered to be indoors—to do the housework, to take care of the children. But that does not mean the father has no responsibility in raising children. We Chinese think that child raising is the most important thing in a family, and mental health is an essential part of it. The children need to know gentleness as well as aggressive feelings. So it is the responsibility of mothers to teach the children what a gentle feeling is, a peaceful feeling rather than an aggressive one. The responsibility of fathers is the opposite. Fathers have to advise the children when there comes a hard time. He teaches them how to fight back with aggressive feelings. In recent years the structure of our society has changed a lot, but the roles in child raising are still unchanged.

Hung-chi Kuo
China (P.R.C.)

ARTICLES

<table>
<tr><td colspan="2">a(n) + noun</td><td colspan="2">the + noun</td></tr>
<tr><td>Singular</td><td>Plural</td><td>Singular</td><td>Plural</td></tr>
<tr><td>a mother</td><td>X mothers</td><td>the mother</td><td>the mothers</td></tr>
<tr><td>a child</td><td>X children</td><td>the child</td><td>the children</td></tr>
<tr><td>an infant</td><td>X infants</td><td>the infant</td><td>the infants</td></tr>
</table>

a(n) + adjective + noun

<table>
<tr><td>Singular</td><td>Plural</td></tr>
<tr><td>a successful father</td><td>X successful fathers</td></tr>
<tr><td>an important job</td><td>X important jobs</td></tr>
</table>

the + adjective + noun

<table>
<tr><td>Singular</td><td>Plural</td></tr>
<tr><td>the successful father</td><td>the successful fathers</td></tr>
<tr><td>the important job</td><td>the important jobs</td></tr>
</table>

EXCEPTIONS

The father brings the money (X) *home.*
The children go to (X) *school.*

The Responsibilities of Raising Children

<u>The</u> father is <u>an</u> important part of <u>the</u> family. First of all, he has to work outside <u>the</u> house to support his family. When he returns <u>X</u> home, he helps <u>the</u> children with their homework, and he asks what they did in <u>X</u> school. On <u>the</u> weekends, he wakes up early, and he takes his children to <u>a</u> movie or to <u>the</u> park. Then he takes them to <u>the</u> store to buy them what they need, like books, clothes, and toys. <u>The</u> father also teaches his children to behave well and to respect other people. He shows them how to be polite, how to talk in <u>a</u> clear voice, and how to pay attention to their teachers. Finally, <u>the</u> father helps his children to be confident and to fight for their rights, even in <u>the</u> worst situations. <u>The</u> father in Libya works more for his children than for himself.

Khadja Al Walda
Libya

> An unkind teacher is better than a kind father.
>
> translated by
> *Adel Salamah*
> Saudi Arabia

Read the paragraphs below. Then do the exercises that follow.

I

Raising Children in France

<u>European culture is male-dominated.</u> This phenomenon appears everywhere, especially in child-raising. <u>The father and mother have two different purposes. The father is the symbol of authority and morality, but the mother gives the children affection and creates a sweet environment without hurt or shock.</u> Usually the place of the mother is more important because the children are in contact with her more than with their father. The father is often gone because his duty is to earn the money which is necessary to raise the children. <u>I think that the mother and father are both important.</u> They approach their children with different feelings and objectives. We cannot say that one is more important for the children. In France, child raising is based on the complementary experiences given by both parents.

Jacques Ferraré
France

1. Circle 12 articles in the paragraph. Underline the nouns (or the adjectives and the nouns) that follow each article.
2. Put 8 prepositional phrases in parentheses.
3. Make the underlined sentences negative.
4. What are the responsibilities of the mother in France? What are the responsibilities of the father?

II

The Roles of Mothers and Fathers

In my country, the roles of the mother and father in raising children
_____ similar. Both parents _____ education, medical
    be   **give**

care, protection, love, and the material things that their children need.
But the difference _____ that the mother _____ the
           be   **have**

responsibility of taking care of the child most of the time at X home.
If a mother _____, she _____ a person to help her
        work   **need**

at X home. The mother _____ food, _____ clothes,
            make   **wash**

_____ the baby, _____ the rules, and _____
   bathe   **teach**   **manage**

the behavior of the children. On the other hand, the father _____
                   work

and _____ the money X home. He _____ his wife
    bring   **help**

with the children at night, but not much. He is interested in his children,
but he _____ no time during the week. On the weekends, when
   have

he _____ at home, he _____ with his children.
 be   **play**

Aleida Perez de Chavez
Venezuela

1. Write the correct form of the present tense verbs in the blanks.
2. Circle 18 articles in the paragraph. Underline the noun (or the adjective and the noun) that follow each article.
3. Put parentheses around 13 prepositional phrases.
4. How is child raising in Venezuela similar to child raising in France (paragraph I)?

___ **INTERVIEW** ___

Ask a friend NOT in your class to describe the responsibilities that mothers and fathers in his or her country have in raising children. Ask your friend some of the questions below to learn more about raising children in that country. Then write a paragraph about your friend's information.

Which parent

> teaches the child to speak?
>
> bathes the child?
>
> punishes the child?
>
> takes the child to school?
>
> takes the child to the doctor?

Is one parent more responsible

> for taking care of the very young child?
>
> for taking care of the older child?
>
> for raising the sons?
>
> for raising the daughters?

Exchange paragraphs with a classmate.

A. Read the paragraph.
B. Circle the articles in the paragraph.
C. Put parentheses around the prepositional phrases.
D. Draw a box around ⌊, and⌋ that joins two clauses.

CONNECTORS

Additional information	*Explanatory information*	*Contrasting information*
also	that is,	but
in addition,	for example,	however,
and	in fact,	
besides X,	for instance,	
in addition to X,		

Pakistani Fathers

The responsibilities of a father start when a child is about five years old. The father takes the child to a proper school, <u>AND</u> he pays the school expenses. He <u>ALSO</u> checks the physical as well as the mental progress of his child, <u>AND</u> he guides the child. <u>IN ADDITION,</u> the father tells his child about the relationships with other family members. Whenever the father gets some time, he takes the child to famous places. On the way, he tells the stories of his ancestors <u>AND</u> thus tries to produce a personality which is according to family traditions. The children will learn from their father, <u>AND</u> they will love him too.

M. Hanif
Pakistan

Read the paragraphs on page 85. Then do the exercises that follow.

I

_____

The responsibilities mothers have in my country _____
be

teaching their children morals, behavior, and discipline. When they

_____ very young, children do not know what is bad and what
be

is good. The mother _____ the person who can tell her children
be

about the bad things and the good things. For instance, when the

mother goes to the grocery store, the child might take something. The

mother must tell the child that if he _____ anything, he must
take

pay for it. If the mother _____ her child telling jokes about an
see

old or a handicapped person, she must scold him. She will also teach

her child to respect and help other people, and she will teach him to

wash his face and to make his bed every day. A good mother can make a

good child by taking the proper responsibility for his behavior.

Parvin Sultana
Bangladesh

_____ EXERCISE 4C _____

1. Write the correct forms of the present tense verbs in the blanks.
2. Underline 3 connectors in the paragraph.
3. Circle 10 articles in the paragraph.
4. Write a title for this paragraph.

II

Fathers in Jordan

Fathers in my country do hard work for their children. First, fathers

take care of their children. For example, they _____ them
buy

clothes, toys, and food. In addition, if a child feels some pain, the father

_____ him to the doctor and _____ medicine for him.
    carry   **buy**

Fathers also _____ their children the importance of education.
                        teach

In fact, this _____ when the child _____ elementary
                    begin   **enter**

school. Second, fathers _____ advice to their children during
                                give

their teenage years. For example, fathers _____ their children
                                                        tell

how to choose friends and how not to be friends with lazy, careless,

drunken, nonreligious students. Fathers also teach their children the

importance of following Islamic rules. A father _____ his son to
                                                        encourage

become educated, to be innocent and active, and to worship Allah. He

_____ his son how to serve Islam by using his talents and by
    teach

sacrificing for his country.

Hasan Al-Mohamed
Jordan

___ EXERCISE 4D _____

1. Write the correct present tense verbs in the blanks.
2. Underline 6 connectors in the paragraph.
3. What do you remember about Hasan's paragraph?
4. What questions could you ask Hasan about this paragraph?

___ WRITING ASSIGNMENT _____

*1. Write two paragraphs. In the first paragraph, write about the
responsibilities that mothers in your country have in raising
children. In the second paragraph, write about the responsibilities fathers in your country have in raising children. Use appropriate connectors in the paragraph. Use the chart below to help
plan your paragraph.*

```
┌─────────────────────────────────────────────────────────────┐
│                                                             │
│       Responsibilities of the Mother in My Country          │
│                                                             │
│   taking care of the child    For example, _____    │
│   teaching the child                                        │
│   ?????????????????????       For instance, _____   │
│                                                             │
│                               For example, _____    │
│                                                             │
│                               In addition, _____    │
│                                                             │
│                               Also, _____     │
│                                                             │
├─────────────────────────────────────────────────────────────┤
│                                                             │
│       Responsibilities of the Father in My Country          │
│                                                             │
│   supporting the child        For example, _____    │
│   teaching the child                                        │
│   ?????????????????????       For instance, _____   │
│                                                             │
│                               For example, _____    │
│                                                             │
│                               In addition, _____    │
│                                                             │
│                               Also, _____     │
│                                                             │
└─────────────────────────────────────────────────────────────┘
```

2. Exchange paragraphs with a classmate. Read each paragraph.

A. In the first paragraph (about mothers' responsibilities), underline the connectors. Then circle the articles.

B. In the second paragraph (about fathers' responsibilities), underline the prepositional phrases. Then circle the noun that follows each preposition.

C. Ask your classmate two questions to learn more about the responsibilities of parents in his or her country.

```
┌─────────────────────────────────────┐
│                                     │
│  God takes his time, but he never   │
│  forgets.                           │
│                                     │
│                    translated by    │
│                    Douglas Chang    │
│                    Ecuador          │
│                                     │
└─────────────────────────────────────┘
```

CHRONOLOGICAL (TIME) CONNECTORS

First, . . .	Before X, . . .	Then, . . .
Second, . . .	After X, . . .	Next, . . .
Third, . . .	During X, . . .	Finally, . . .
	Afterwards, . . .	

How to Cook One of My Favorite Foods

I'm going to write about how to cook chicken gizzards. FIRST, you have to wash and cut the chicken gizzards. SECOND, you have to put them into the pot. Do not add water because the chicken gizzards have their own water. THEN cook the gizzards. AFTER the liquid decreases, put one glass of hot water into the pot. You have to repeat that twice. THIRD, when the chicken gizzards are soft, you need to cut onion and to fry it. THEN you put the fried onion in the pot with the chicken gizzards. AFTER THAT, add salt and pepper. FINALLY, you have one plate of excellent chicken gizzards.

Maria M. Lopez
Colombia

Eating is more important than looking at pretty blossoms.

translated by
Mari Kaneda
Japan

Read the paragraphs below. Then do the exercises that follow.

I

Cooking Spaghetti

It is easy to learn how to make spaghetti. First, I put some water, salt, and oil in a pan. Then I put the pan on the stove for about 15 minutes. After this, I put the spaghetti into the pan for ten minutes. Then I take the pan off the stove. After that, I <u>put</u> tomato juice, oil, salt, and meat in another pan. I <u>cook</u> these ingredients on the stove for half an hour. After a while, I <u>take</u> the spaghetti out of the pan, and I <u>serve</u> it. I <u>put</u> the sauce on top of the spaghetti, and I <u>serve</u> it with cheese.

Mariam Peaspán
Italy

_____ EXERCISE 4E _____

1. Rewrite the paragraph. Substitute "she" for "I." Remember to change the underlined present tense verbs to agree with the new subject:

I <u>put</u> → she <u>puts</u>

2. Put parentheses around the prepositional phrases. Circle the noun that follows each preposition.

3. Underline 6 chronological (time) connectors.

4. Could you make spaghetti by following the directions in Miriam's paragraph? What questions could you ask her?

I

How to Make Rice

I <u>make</u> rice almost every day. First, I <u>put</u> some water in a pot. ∗ Then I <u>put</u> the pot on the fire. When it becomes hot, I <u>add</u> some salt to it. Second, I <u>put</u> rice in the pot that contains the water. Third, I <u>add</u> some butter. ∗ I <u>cook</u> the rice over a medium fire for about 15 minutes. Finally, the rice is ready. ∗ I <u>serve</u> it to my guests.

Ahmed Badahdah
Saudi Arabia

_____ EXERCISE 4F _____

1. Rewrite Ahmed's paragraph. Change each "I" to "he." Change the underlined present tense verbs to agree with the new subject.

2. Join two clauses with ⌐, and⌐ where you see the asterisk (∗).

3. Underline 5 chronological connectors.

4. Could you make rice by following Ahmed's directions? What questions could you ask him?

___ WRITING ASSIGNMENT _____

Read the recipe below. Then write a paragraph that tells a friend how to make that recipe. Use chronological connectors. The meanings of the abbreviations are:

T. = tablespoon

t. = teaspoon

Scrambled Eggs

1–2 T. butter   1. Melt in a pan over low heat
3 eggs   2. Beat with a fork until the
                      eggs are thoroughly mixed

Add and mix into the eggs:
¼ t. salt
⅛ t. paprika
2 T. milk or cream

Optional additions:
grated cheese
chopped tomatoes
chopped onion
sautéed mushrooms

Pour the mixture into the pan. Cook slowly, turning the eggs with a spoon until the mixture thickens. Makes two servings.

Show your paragraph about scrambled eggs to a friend who is NOT in your class. Does your friend understand each step? Does he or she have questions that must be answered to complete the recipe? Add any necessary information to your paragraph.

(you +) **Root Form of the Verb + Complement.**

*Mix** the ingredients.
*Bake** the cake.
*Be** careful.
*Go** to the oven.
*Serve** the guests.
*Sit** down.

NOTE: The root form of the verb is used in the imperative.

How to Bake a Cake

I like cakes, and they are easy to bake. First, <u>READ</u> the recipe carefully. Then <u>GATHER</u> the ingredients and <u>TURN</u> on the oven to 350 degrees F. After that, <u>MIX</u> the sugar with the butter. <u>ADD</u> the flour and <u>CONTINUE</u> mixing for fifteen minutes. Next, <u>TURN</u> off the beater and <u>POUR</u> the mixture into a cake pan. After that, <u>PUT</u> the cake in the oven. Finally, after half-an-hour, <u>CHECK</u> to see if the cake is ready, and <u>TAKE</u> the cake out of the oven.

Yusmary Espinoza
Venezuela

Read the paragraphs below. Then do the exercises that follow.

I

Kabsa

It is not difficult to make Kabsa. First, you need a pot, water, rice, onion, tomato and some spices. To cook the kabsa, fry the onion for two minutes. <u>Then add the tomato with some salt and spices.</u> After that, pour in some water. The amount of water should be double the rice. For example, if you are going to use one cup of rice, use two cups of water. <u>After a while, add the rice and put the lid on the pot for thirty minutes.</u> After that, you will find that a delicious dish is waiting for you to enjoy.

Fares El-Ja
Kuwait

1. Underline 6 imperatives in the paragraph.
2. Circle 6 chronological connectors.
3. Make the underlined sentences negative.
4. Could you make Kabsa by following Fares' instructions? What questions could you ask Fares about his recipe?

II

Making Caipiriuha

Follow these steps, and you will have a typical Brazilian drink called Caipiriuha. First, buy the ingredients: cachac'a (a Brazilian alcoholic beverage made out of sugar cane), lemon, and sugar. If you cannot find cachac'a, vodka will do. After that, start the mixing. Squeeze 4 lemons and mix them with ½ cup of water. Then put this mixture in a jar with two cups of cachac'a, and mix them very well. Finally, add some crushed ice. Then taste it. Modify the amount of each ingredient according to your taste. Before serving the drink, put a slice of lemon in each glass to make it more appealing. Serve Caipiriuha in large glasses, and enjoy it!

Marluce Albuquerque
Brazil

—— Exercise 4H ——

1. Underline 10 imperative verbs in the paragraph.
2. Circle 4 chronological connectors.
3. Put parentheses around 7 articles.
4. Could you make this recipe by following Marluce's instructions? What questions could you ask Marluce about her recipe?

> The person who has bread doesn't have teeth,
> and the person who has teeth doesn't have bread.
>
> translated by
> *Semoa de Sousa*
> Sao Tomé, West Africa

1. Write a paragraph about how to cook a food from your country. Answer some of the following questions.

What is the food?

What are the ingredients?

How much of each ingredient do you use?

What steps do you follow to cook the food?

First, . . .

Second, . . .

After that, . . .

How long does each step take?

How does the food smell? Taste?

2. Exchange paragraphs with a classmate. Read the paragraph. Could you make that food? Ask your classmate any necessary questions to complete the recipe.

__ **WRITING ASSIGNMENT** _____

Look at the chart on page 94 that describes the kinds of international restaurants most liked by North Americans. Then write a paragraph that describes the chart. Answer some of the questions below.

What percentage of Americans like Italian food?

What percentage of Americans like Chinese food?

What percentage of Americans like the other kinds of food on the chart?

Why do Americans like these international foods?

What international foods do people in your country like? Why?

Use some of the following sentences to write your paragraph:

According to the National Restaurant Association, . . .

more than . . . Americans like X.

many Americans also like X.

in addition, _____% of Americans like X.

some Americans, _____%, like X.

a few Americans, _____%, like X.

I think Americans like international food because . . .

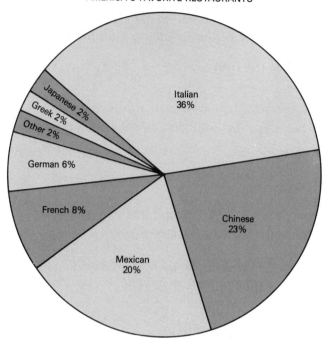

AMERICA'S FAVORITE RESTAURANTS

Italian 36%

Chinese 23%

Mexican 20%

French 8%

German 6%

Other 2%

Greek 2%

Japanese 2%

Do not be either too soft, or you will be kneaded, or too hard, for you will be broken.

translated by
Adel Salamah
Iran

JOINING CLAUSES WITH CONNECTORS

ADDITIONAL INFORMATION

S + V (+C) [, and] S + V (+C).

CONTRASTING INFORMATION

S + V (+ C) [, but] S + V (+ C).

CAUSE-EFFECT INFORMATION

S + V (+ C) [, so] S + V (+ C).

> I love you O' my heartbeat.
> I love you O' best love in my life.
> Your love is my destination.
> You love is my hope.
> Although life separated us,
> You are close to me.
>
> translated by
> *Hassan Hareeri*
> Saudi Arabia

Wedding Customs in Iran

There are three phases that Iranians usually follow when a man and a woman get married. First, a man chooses a girl, and then he has to talk with his parents. If his parents are satisfied with the future bride, they arrange to meet the girl's parents. The man and his parents put on new clothing , AND they go to the girl's home. They discuss the marriage with the girl's parents , BUT the girl is not present. Afterwards, if the girl and her parents are pleased with the man, the girl brings tea and sweets for the guests , SO the man and the girl see each other. Then the man's father and the girl's father talk about the amount of the dowry , AND the man's mother and the girl's mother discuss the time of the engagement party. Finally, the man puts the engagement ring on the girl's finger.

Mahmoud Shafaibajestan
Iran

Read the paragraphs below. Then do the exercises that follow.

I

Marriage in Jordan

Marriage in my country has specific steps. The first of these is the age of the groom. He should be over twenty years old. Second, the groom must cover the requirements of the bride such as clothes, gold, and the wedding ceremony, so he must have a lot of money. Then the groom thinks about a suitable wife for himself. He looks for many things such as her culture, her beauty, her family, and her age, so the process takes a long time. After that, he finds a suitable wife, and he talks with his family. It is very important to

have the blessing of his family. If he and his family agree, they go to the father of the bride who has the power to give them the final decision. Finally,
the two families agree on the marriage, and they plan the bridal day and the
ceremony.

Basem Masaedeh
Jordan

___ EXERCISE 41 _____

1. Put parentheses ( ) around 5 time connectors in the paragraph.
2. Circle the subject (S) and the verb (V) in the underlined sentences.
3. Put brackets [ ] around the [, and] and the [, so] that join two
   clauses.
4. What questions could you ask Basem about marriage in his country? What could he write another paragraph about?

II

Marriage Customs in Honduras

There are many steps to follow when two persons decide to get married
in Honduras. First, there is an engagement that begins when the groom's
parents ask the bride's parents for her hand. The groom always gives his
bride a ring as a symbol of their union until they get married. For the
engagement party, the man usually wears a suit. * The girl wears a beautiful pastel dress. This event usually takes place in the bride's house. * All
the relatives of the young couple are invited. After that, there is a civil marriage in the District Center. * A few months after the civil marriage, the
church ceremony takes place. The civil ceremony is performed by a
lawyer. * The church ceremony is performed by a priest. In this ceremony,
the young couple is united before God. * This is the most important part of
the marriage. The clothes worn by the young couple are special clothes. The
girl wears a long white dress with a veil covering her face. * The man wears
a black or a white suit. Afterwards, the parents of the groom give a big party
for all the relatives and friends of the young couple. Finally, the bride and
the groom go on a trip for their honeymoon.

Olga Handal
Honduras

1. Join two clauses with [, and], [, but], or [, so] where you see the asterisks (*).
2. Underline 3 connectors in the paragraph.
3. Put parentheses around three adverbs of frequency.
4. Circle THERE IS and THERE ARE in the paragraph. Put the subjects of THERE IS and THERE ARE in brackets [ ].

> The first time I saw your face,
> I felt it was the passing wind.
> Now I know it is yearning for you.
> When I trace your shadow,
> when I see your face,
> I belong to you.
>
> translated by
> *Woo Seok Cheon*
> Korea

—— **WRITING ASSIGNMENT** ————————————

Write THREE paragraphs about marriage in your country. Answer some of the questions below.

Paragraph I: *How People in My Country Become Engaged*

Do the men and women in your country decide whom they should marry?

Do the parents in your country decide whom their sons and daughters should marry?

How is an engagement arranged? (First, Then, After that, Finally)

Paragraph II: *How the Bride Prepares for the Wedding*

How long is the engagement period?

Who helps the bride plan the wedding?

What plans are made? (First, Then, Afterwards, Finally)

Where is the wedding held?

Who is invited to the wedding?

Paragraph III: *The Wedding Day*

What do the bride and groom wear?

What happens on that day? (First, Second, Next, After that, Finally)

What special foods are served?

What special customs occur?

Appearing in her eyes there was a tear,
and on my lips, a forgiving phrase.
Pride spoke, and she dried her tear,
and the phrase on my lips expired.
I follow one road, she follows another,
but when thinking of our mutual love
I say even now, "Why didn't I speak that day?"
And she would say, "Why didn't I cry?"

translated by
Gustavo Garcia
Ecuador

Read the paragraphs below. Then do the exercises that follow.

I

My Country

Japan consists of four large islands and more than 300 small islands. The largest island _____ Honshu. It is in the center. To the north _____ Hokkaido. * To the southwest are Shikoku and Kyushu. Tokyo _____ the capital of Japan. It _____ on the island of Honshu. Tokyo is a very big city. * It has many companies. About eight million people live in Tokyo. The most famous mountain in Japan is Mount Fujiyama. It _____ 12,388 feet high. From the top of Mount Fuji, one can see the city of Tokyo. Other large cities in Japan _____ Osaka, Sapporo, Yokohama, and Nagasaki. Each of these cities has famous shrines and historical places.

Akiko Kudo
Japan

1. Write the correct form of the verb TO BE in the blanks.
2. Join two clauses with [, and] where you see the asterisk (∗).
3. Put parentheses ( ) around five prepositional phrases.
4. What questions could you ask Akiko about Japan? What other paragraphs could Akiko write about Japan?

CAMBODIA (Kampuchea)

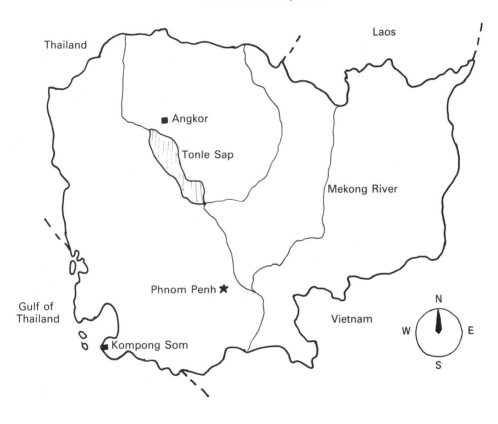

II

The Climate and the Crops in Cambodia

Cambodia is a small country located in Southeast Asia. The land surface is flat. ∗ Mountains surround its borders. The mountains have jungles which are full of plants and wild animals. In Cambodia there are two types of weather: hot and rainy. During the winter, the heavy rainfall and the warm temperatures are just right for growing rice. * Most people in Cambodia work on their farms during the whole season. <u>They take care of the plants until the summer.</u> During the hot weather, the people collect their rice from the fields. * They put it in the supply house. If they make a lot of rice, they keep only enough for their family. They sell the rest to the government because they need the money to buy some things. However, people in Cambodia also grow vegetables, tobacco, or anything they need. In the summer, the farm work is finished. * Some people visit their relatives for a few months. I like the hot weather in my country. * I also like the rain that makes everything grow.

Farid Soeu
Cambodia

___ EXERCISE 4L ___

1. Join two clauses with [, and] , [, so] , or [, but] where you see the asterisk (*).
2. Circle the subject (S) and the verb (V) in the underlined sentences.
3. How does Farid's map help you to understand his paragraph?
4. Write two questions that you could ask Farid about Cambodia. What other paragraphs could he write about his country?

II

The Geography of Honduras

Honduras is a small country with many interesting geographical areas and a tropical climate. <u>The population in Honduras is about 4 million inhabitants.</u> * <u>It has a total area of 43,277 square miles.</u> It has many rivers and mountains. The most important and largest rivers are the Ulve and the Patuca. The highest and the most important mountains are the Cordillera de Merendon in the west and the Cordillera de Agalta in the northeast of the country. The seasons are not marked. For example, Honduras does not get snow at all. * The lowest temperature ever recorded was zero degrees F. Almost all year it is summer on the coast and spring in the rest of the country. <u>In the center of Honduras, the winds blow often.</u> * <u>The temperature changes very often.</u> There is only one large lake in Honduras. It is called Lago de Yojoa. * It is located in the west, between two important cities, Santa Barbara and Siguatepeque. In addition, Honduras has many forests. Honduras is a beautiful country. * I am happy that it is my country.

Olga Handal
Honduras

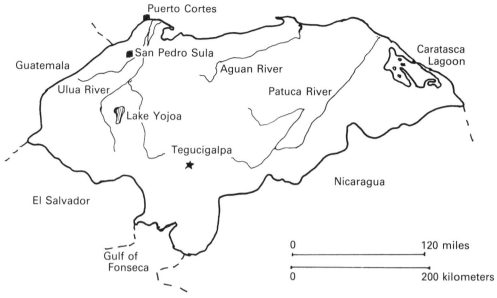

Carribbean Sea

Puerto Cortes

San Pedro Sula

Guatemala

Aguan River

Caratasca Lagoon

Ulua River

Patuca River

Lake Yojoa

Tegucigalpa

★

Nicaragua

El Salvador

Gulf of
Fonseca

Pacific Ocean

0   120 miles

0   200 kilometers

___ EXERCISE 4M ___

1. Join two clauses with `, and` or `, so` where you see the asterisks (*).

2. Make the underlined clauses negative.

3. How does Olga's map help you understand her paragraph?

4. What questions could you ask Olga about her country? What other paragraphs could she write about her country?

Song of Five Friends

How many friends have I? Count them:
Water and stone, pine and bamboo,
the rising moon on the east mountain.
I welcome the moon—it too is my friend.
What need is there, I say, to have more friends than five?

translated by
Chul Lee
Korea

Make a map of your country and the countries or seas surrounding it. Put the major cities, major rivers and lakes, and major mountains and deserts on the map. Then write THREE paragraphs about your country. Use some of the topics below.

The Geography of My Country

The Rivers of My Country

A Famous Desert in My Country

The Most Famous Mountain in My Country

The Largest City in My Country

The Political System in My Country

An Important Crop in My Country

A Place Tourists Visit in My Country

A City for Vacationing in My Country

To plan your paragraph, use a chart like the two on these pages:

AN IMPORTANT CROP IN MY COUNTRY

MAJOR RIVERS IN MY COUNTRY

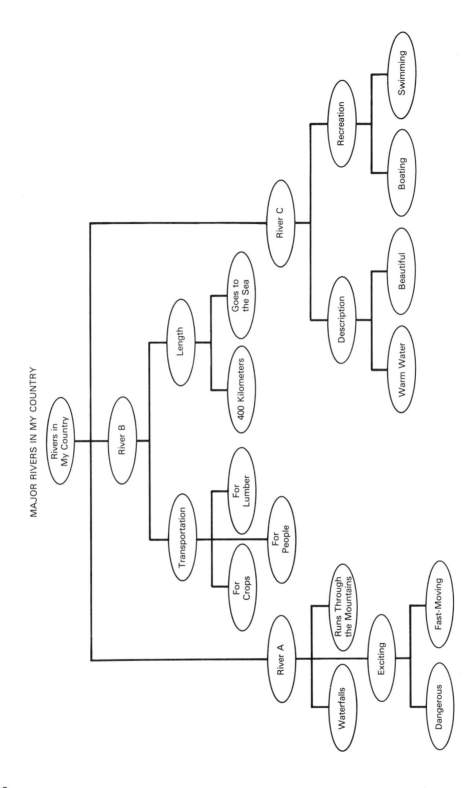

My Favorite Dinner in My Country

Party Food in My Country

Beverages in My Country

My Favorite Restaurant

A Game Children Play in My Country

WRITING PROJECTS

Individual Project

Make a booklet about your country. Use the paragraph(s) that you wrote for the assignment above. Write some additional paragraphs about additional places in your country. Write about some of the paragraph topics below.

A Small Town in My Country

The Largest City in My Country

My Favorite Vacation Place in My Country

A Famous Historical Place in My Country

The Most Beautiful Place in My Country

A Place Where Many Tourists Go in My Country

A Place Where Tourists Do Not Go in My Country

Decorate your booklet with drawings, maps, and photographs about your country. Ask the Office of International Services to display your booklet during International Week, or present the booklet to the public library.

Group Project

Make a recipe booklet of international foods. Collect recipes and directions for cooking the foods from classmates and friends. Put a list of cooking abbreviations at the beginning of the booklet. Make a table of contents for the booklets: list the name of each recipe and the page on which it appears. Use illustrations to demonstrate some of the tasks. Decorate the recipe book with drawings or photographs. Then have a party for the class, and cook the foods. Present a copy of the recipe booklet to the local or the university newspaper. Give permission to print the recipes in the newspaper.

Five

Travel Experiences

Preparing for My Trip

On August 6, the *New Nigerian Newspaper* listed me as a participant in an educational training program, so I quickly prepared to travel. At that time, my country banned new passports, but I went to the Ministry of Education in Lagos, Nigeria. The minister issued me a passport and other documents. Then I went to the American Embassy in Lagos, and the people there were very helpful. After that, I returned to my village to inform my parents and other relatives about my trip, and they all prayed for me. On August 25, I finally boarded the plane for my new life.

Sanni B. Mounde
Nigeria

PAST TENSE (-ed) SPELLING FOR REGULAR VERBS*

consonant + e (d)	**1 vowel + 1 consonant** **(double the final consonant + -ed)**
prepa*re* → prepare*d* arri*ve* → arrive*d*	st*op* → stop*ped* trav*el* → trave*lled*
2 Consonants (-ed)	**2 Vowels + 1 consonant (-ed)**
fini*sh* → finish*ed* wa*lk* → walk*ed*	n*eed* → need*ed* w*ait* → wait*ed*
Consonant + y (y -ied)	**Vowel + y (-ed)**
stu*dy* → stud*ied* wor*ry* → worr*ied*	enj*oy* → enjoy*ed* pl*ay* → play*ed*

*NOTE: See the inside front cover of this book for spelling rules.

The moon of foreign countries is bigger than the moon in our own country.

translated by
Hsiang-Rwei Tseng
Taiwan (R.O.C.)

How I Prepared for a Trip

Last year, I <u>prepared</u> carefully for my vacation trip. First, I <u>wanted</u> to know more about the city, so I <u>asked</u> my friends about it. Then I made my travel reservations, and I <u>counted</u> my money. Next, I <u>packed</u> my camera and my clothes. Finally, I <u>looked</u> at some pictures, and I <u>studied</u> a map of the city.

Harijano Tedjo
Indonesia

Read the paragraphs below. Write the correct form of the past tense verbs in the blanks. Then do the exercises that follow.

I

Preparing for a Trip

Before I came to the United States, I _____ very busy
               be

preparing for all the things that I _____. It took about a month
              need

for me to get ready. First, I went to Kuala Lumpur (that is the capital

city of Malaysia) to get a visa. <u>My sponsor gave me important documents.</u>

After that, I _____ to my town, and I _____ the doctor
       return   **visit**

for a medical check-up. <u>The doctor gave me a health certificate.</u> My

mother was also busy making dresses for me. <u>She _____ a lot of</u>
                             sew

<u>dresses.</u> I also bought some <u>books in my language.</u> <u>For example, I bought

a dictionary and some religious books.</u> Besides that I _____
                                    pack

some spices and preserved food. <u>Finally, I _____ my relatives to</u>
                                 visit

<u>say goodbye.</u>

Noorazian Ariffin
Malaysia

1. Identify the subjects (S) and the verbs (V) in the underlined sentences.
2. Circle 5 connectors in the paragraph.
3. What do you remember about the paragraph?
4. Is the writer male or female? How do you know?

II

Preparing for My Trip to the Philippines

Before I left Sri Lanka to travel to the Philippines, I _____
have

to make certain preparations. First, I _____ my passport,
obtain

visa, medical documents, air ticket, and traveller's checks. Then I

_____ the materials I would need, such as clothes, writing
gather

materials, and books. After that, I made a list, and I _____
pack

all the needed things in bags. I also _____ mentally for my trip.
prepare

I told myself, "When you are there, maybe no one will be friendly to you.
If you are rejected, can you stand it?" My mental answer _____
be

that I could. So I found a strong and favorable mental attitude that
helped me to remain happy in a new country that is very different from
my country.

I. M. Gunawardena
Sri Lanka

— EXERCISE 5B

1. Identify the subjects (S) and the verbs (V) in the underlined sentences.
2. Underline 3 time connectors in the paragraph.
3. What is the main idea in the paragraph? How do you know?
4. What was the most important preparation made by the author? How do you know?

III

_____

When I _____ my admission from a university in the United
          receive

States, I _____ very happy. I tried to become as informed as
            be

possible about the American lifestyle. First, I _____ to foreign
                                                    talk

people who had visited the U.S.A., and I _____ to U.S. radio
                                              listen

stations. Of course, I also wrote a few letters to some Moroccan students

in the U.S. I _____ that the U.S. had chilly weather, so I bought
                  learn

some heavy coats, and my mother _____ some medicines
                                      pack

and hot spices to prevent illness. Then I _____ to bring some
                                              decide

typical and traditional things with me like Moroccan songs, clothes, and

my family pictures. I also _____ English a little. After that, I
                              study

_____ all my administrative papers. Finally, I went to three
    obtain

different cities to say goodbye to some of my closest friends.

M'Hamed Jebbanema
Morocco

___ EXERCISE 5C _____

1. Put boxes around the ⌐, and⌐ and ⌐, so⌐ that join two clauses.
   Circle the subjects in each of the clauses.

2. Underline 5 time connectors.

3. Write a title for the paragraph.

4. Why did the author take some traditional things with him to the
   U.S.?

Read the paragraphs below. Then do the exercises that follow.

I

Preparing for a Trip

When I came to the UPLB in the Philippines, I first _____
receive

a visa from the Philippine Embassy in Thailand. Then I _____
prepare

the papers for my field of study, and I _____ my friend who was
contact

studying at UPLB. After that, I _____ my personal belongings. I
prepare

did not bring a suit and a necktie because in the Philippines, people

usually use informal dress like the American style. The Thai foods that I

brought were dry chili, dry sweet pork, Thai chili sauce, and some dry

desserts. I also _____ some Thai souvenirs, cigarette cases and
pack

ladies' necklaces, for my advisory committee and my Philippino friends.

Finally, I met respected relatives to say goodbye, and I _____
receive

some good wishes from them. The day I left, I paid respect to my Lord

Buddha, and my parents took photographs of my family and the people

who came to the airport.

Samakkee Boonyawat
Thailand

1. Write the correct past tense verbs in the blanks.
2. Circle the articles in the paragraph.
3. Put boxes around the ⌐, and⌐ that joins two clauses. Underline the subject in each of the clauses in those sentences.
4. Why did the author pack some souvenirs?

II

Preparing for My Future

I was awarded a fellowship, so I _____ to study in the
                             decide

United States of America. However, I _____ about three things.
                                worry

First, my friends told me about the cold winter, so I _____ a
                                   purchase

few winter clothes. Secondly, I _____ for my family to stay in
                          arrange

India for the year I would be gone. Third, I am a vegetarian, and I was

afraid that I would not be able to eat as I travelled, so I _____
                                 pack

some food for my journey.

Ashok Kumar Hebbar
India

1. Write the correct past tense verbs in the blanks.
2. Put parentheses around 5 prepositional phrases in the paragraph. Circle the noun (or the pronoun) that follows each preposition.
3. Put boxes around ⌐, and⌐ and ⌐, so⌐ in the paragraph. Underline the subject for each of the clauses in those sentences.
4. What questions could you ask the author about the preparations he made for his trip? What other paragraphs could he write?

Write a paragraph describing your preparations for a long trip. Use the chart below to plan your paragraph. Use [. and] *,* [. but] *, or* [. so] *to join two clauses in several of the sentences.*

How I Prepared for a Long Trip

First, I _____

Second, I _____

Then I _____

After that, I _____

Next, I _____

Then I _____

Finally, I _____

Exchange paragraphs with a classmate. Read that paragraph. Ask your classmate two questions about his or her preparation. Then:

    A. Underline the past tense verbs.

    B. Put each prepositional phrase in parentheses.

    C. Put boxes around each [. and] , [. but] , and [. so] joining two clauses.

    D. Circle the connectors in the paragraph.

My life, which was like two or three days, is gone,
as fast as the water in the brook
and the wind in the valley.
I never worry about two days:
the day which has gone,
and the day which is not here yet.

translated by
Keyvan Karbassiyon
Iran

IRREGULAR VERBS—PAST TENSE (EXAMPLES)*

Present	Past	Present	Past
begin	began	know	knew
break	broke	leave	left
bring	brought	make	made
buy	bought	say	said
come	came	see	saw
feel	felt	sit	sat
find	found	speak	spoke
fly	flew	stand	stood
get	got	spend	spent
give	gave	take	took
go	went	tell	told
hang	hung		

*NOTE: See Appendix A for a list of regular and irregular verbs.

Preparing for a Long Trip

Like almost all men in our traditional African society, I prepared for the major trip which led me out of my country by informing the people in my village. First, as our customs require, I visited the chief of the village, and I informed him about my decision to leave for another country. He GAVE me permission to go, and he advised me not to forget the relatives I was about to leave. What I did next was to consult the Imam of the mosque. Since I acted according to tradition, I BROUGHT him some cola nuts, and he blessed me by reading some verses from the Koran. After that, I WENT from family to family, and I TOLD them that I was planning to travel. Those who had some relatives in the country I was going to GAVE me letters and asked me to transmit their greetings to their relatives. Thus, I fulfilled the conditions which all men in our society must fulfill before travelling, and I LEFT for my first long trip.

Cheick F. M. Kanté
Mali

If you don't go to the tiger's cave,
how can you catch the cub?

translated by
Prayat Laoprapossone
Thailand

Read the paragraphs below. Write the present tense verb *ABOVE each of the underlined past tense irregular verbs. Then do the exercises that follow.*

I

An Adventure!

When I was flying from Magadisho Airport to the U.S., I <u>felt</u> very nervous, and I was so sad about leaving my family. It <u>was</u> not the first time for me to fly in an airplane, but it was the longest trip that I had taken. However, it was an adventure for me to fly for over twenty hours. For example, I was amazed when I experienced jet lag between my country and the U.S.A., and I also experienced it between New York and Missouri. Since it was a very long trip, I felt light-headed. I also <u>felt</u> my ears popping, and, of course, I experienced motion sickness. In fact, when I arrived in the U.S.A., I <u>was</u> so tired that I slept almost three days!

Abdirizak Osman
Somalia

____ EXERCISE 5F _____

    1. Circle the subject for the underlined irregular past tense verbs.
    2. Put boxes around the ⌊, and⌋ and ⌊, but⌋ that join two clauses.
    3. Put parentheses around 5 articles.
    4. Why did Abdirizak sleep for nearly three days?

II

When I Flew to the U.S.A.

On the afternoon of September 8, I <u>took</u> an airplane and left my country, Taiwan. First I <u>flew</u> to Japan, and I stayed there about one hour. * Then I transferred to another airplane to go to San Francisco. I was sitting between two Chinese men. * I did not have any conversation with these neighbors. I was overwhelmed with grief and apprehension about leaving my mother and my boyfriend. As the airplane flew through the air, I <u>held</u> back my tears and tried to read. * I <u>felt</u> uncomfortable and nauseous. I <u>spent</u> about fourteen hours in the airplane. * I could not sleep because it was too terrible. Although I was going to a new place, I felt anxious and queasy. All in all, I think my flight to the United States <u>was</u> a bad experience.

Hui-Ching Chiang
Taiwan (R.O.C.)

_____ EXERCISE 5G _____

1. Circle the subject for the underlined irregular past tense verbs.
2. Write ⎡, and⎤ or ⎡, but⎤ to join two clauses where you see the asterisks (*).
3. Put parentheses around 2 negative verbs in the paragraph.
4. Why was Hui-Ching's flight a bad experience for her?

_____ INTERVIEW _____

Ask a person NOT in your class to describe a trip that he or she took. Use the questions below to help plan the interview:

What did you do first?

What did you do next?

Then what did you do?

After that, what did you do?

Ask your friend any other necessary questions to complete the paragraph. Then write the paragraph about your friend's preparations. Use regular and irregular past tense verbs, and use time connectors. In some sentences, join two clauses with ⎡, and⎤ , ⎡, but⎤ , *or* ⎡, so⎤ .

Exchange paragraphs with a classmate. Read that paragraph. Then:

A. Underline the regular and irregular past tense verbs.
B. Circle the subject pronouns.
C. Put boxes around the ⎡, and⎤ , ⎡, but⎤ , or ⎡, so⎤ that joins two clauses.
D. Are there questions you could ask your classmate about the paragraph?

VERBS OF FEELING + ADJECTIVES

	Present			**Past**	
	Verb	*Adjective*		*Verb*	*Adjective*
I	feel	happy.	I	felt	(very) lonely.
He She It }	seems	frightened.	He She It }	seemed	unhappy.
You	look (very)	angry.	You	looked	sick.
We	become	apprehensive.	We	became	sad.
They	are	kind.	They	were	tired.

Leaving

Before I left my country to come to the U.S.A., I WAS very UNCOM-FORTABLE because I had to leave my family. When I was at the airport, I WAS APPREHENSIVE because this was the first time I was going to leave my family. After I said goodbye to my family, I went to the airplane, but I FELT UNHAPPY. At the moment that the airplane was starting to move, I FELT TERRIBLE. When the airplane was in the air, I saw my country through the window. It LOOKED so SMALL that it looked like a map. The flight attendant gave me my food and a cup of tea. After that, I took a nap. When I woke up, I found myself in Washington. I WAS AMAZED because the time went by so fast. At the same time, I FELT COLD, SCARED, and HOMESICK already.

Ameen Alawi
United Arab Emirates

Read the paragraphs on pages 117–118. Then do the exercises that follow.

I

Leaving My Family

I do not want to think about the day I left my country. I felt sad about leaving my family and my friends. * It was a very bad day. I wanted to stay with them. * The airplane was waiting for me. My body felt tight because I did not want to leave. I saw my family. * I began to think, "Is this the way I should follow or not? What will happen to me when I leave my family?" Before this trip, I had travelled for just a few weeks. * This time I was not returning for five years or more. My mother was very sad. * I held her because I did not want her to cry. I held my father, my brothers, and my sisters. Then I said goodbye.

Mohamed Gaddah
Morocco

___ EXERCISE 5H ___

1. Underline 3 verbs of feeling + the adjectives in the paragraph.

2. Put parentheses around 3 negative verbs in the paragraph.

3. Write the [, and], [, but], or [, so] that joins two clauses where you see the asterisks (*).

4. How long will Mohamed be separated from his family?

II

The Miami Airport

When I arrived at the airport in Miami, it was the night before Christmas. First, I looked for a telephone to call my friend. * I got lost. I became frightened. When I tried to ask for help, the people did not understand me, so I felt frustrated. Finally, I found a telephone. * I called my friend. However, she told me that she could not pick me up because she was sick. I felt so sad and lonely. Then I spent Christmas eve and Christmas morning at the Miami airport. I was very angry. * I wanted to go back to my country.

Silvia C. Higuera
Colombia

___ EXERCISE 5I ___

1. Underline 4 verbs + adjectives of feeling in the paragraph.

2. Circle 4 regular past tense verbs.

3. Join two clauses with `, and` , `, but` , or `, so` where you see the asterisks.

4. Why did Silvia want to return to Colombia?

III

Angry and Happy

After the plane landed in Tucson, Arizona, I _____ to
                                                    want

telephone my parents' friends, but I did not know the spelling of their

last name. I _____ the operator, and I _____ my
              call   **explain**

problem. She said, "I cannot give you a telephone number if you do not

know the spelling of the last name." Then I _____, "I think that
                                              say

the first letter is Y." She said, "I do not know. I do not know." Then

she _____ up. That _____ me so angry. After that, I
     hang   **make**

_____ very anxious, but I _____ to try again. This
 feel   **decide**

time, the new operator _____ very kind, and she _____
                        be   **speak**

Spanish! I _____ very happy to hear her voice, and she
            be

_____ me locate my parents' friends.
 help

Sandra Fuñes
El Salvador

--- EXERCISE 5J _____

1. Write the correct regular and irregular past tense verbs in the blanks.
2. Circle 5 negative verbs in the paragraph.
3. Put parentheses around 4 connectors.
4. Why is the title of this paragraph "Angry and Happy"?

NEGATIVE PAST TENSE*

Regular Verbs

I	want**ed**	I	**did not** want
He She It	visit**ed**	He She It	**did not** visit
You	stud**ied**	*You*	**did not** study
We	stay**ed**	We	**did not** stay
They	help**ed**	They	**did not** help

Irregular Verbs

I	*came*	I	**did not** come
He She It	*went*	He She It	**did not** go
You	*wrote*	You	**did not** write
We	*had*	We	**did not** have
They	*did*	They	**did not** do

*NOTE: The root form of the verb is used with negative past tense.

Lost!

I arrived at J. F. Kennedy Airport with a group of Finnish students, and we <u>DID NOT KNOW</u> where to go. We <u>DID NOT FIND</u> the terminal for our connecting flight. We asked some people, but they <u>DID NOT UNDERSTAND</u> us. The airport was as big as a city, but we finally found our flight. When we arrived in Washington, D.C., we <u>DID NOT KNOW</u> how to reach the hotel. The street system was so different, and there were so many people. Some of the people were nice to us, so we found our hotel. We <u>DID NOT HAVE</u> to sleep on the street!

Katrina Lahtinen
Finland

Ask a person NOT in your class to describe his or her feelings when he or she took an airplane trip. Ask some of the questions below:

How did you feel at first?

How did you feel at the airport?

How did you feel when the plane took off?

How did you feel during the flight?

How did you feel after that?

How did you feel when you arrived at your destination?

Write a paragraph about that person's feelings. Use correct object and subject pronouns. Use regular and irregular past tense verbs, and use connectors. In some sentences, join two clauses with `, and` , `, but` , *or* `, so` . *If necessary, use negative past tense.*

Exchange paragraphs with a classmate. Read the paragraph.

A. Underline the regular and irregular past tense verbs.

B. Put a box around the `, and` , `, but` , or `, so` that joins two clauses.

C. Circle the verbs of feeling + the adjectives.

D. Are there any questions you could ask your classmate about the paragraph?

One time of seeing is better than one hundred times of asking.

translated by
Kyu-Yong Lee
Korea

Read the paragraphs on pages 121–123. Then do the exercises that follow.

I

Our Arrival in the United States

My family _____ from Vietnam. We _____ to the
　　　　　　　　　escape　　　　　　　　　　　　　　**fly**

United States safely from the enemies below us. Many of the airplanes

trying to escape _____ shot down, but our airplane did not get
　　　　　　　　　be

caught. God _____ us through safely. After we arrived, we
　　　　　　　help

_____ to an immigrant camp in Arkansas. We did not plan to
　　go

stay there. It _____ a camp for immigrants to live until they
　　　　　　　　be

_____ their friends, family, or sponsor. Even though my own
　　contact

people _____ all around me, I did not feel comfortable. However,
　　　　　be

my family was lucky to get the best room in the apartment. It was the

only room that had a door and privacy. Other rooms _____
　　　　　　　　　　　　　　　　　　　　　　　　　　　　have

wooden walls that did not reach to the ceiling, but just _____
　　　　　　　　　　　　　　　　　　　　　　　　　　　　divide

them into little compartments. That first week _____ an
　　　　　　　　　　　　　　　　　　　　　be

experience for me. I _____ new things to expect in the United
　　　　　　　　learn

States, and I also _____ to speak the American language. One
　　　　　　　　　begin

thing that I was sad about was that my father was not there to share the

experience.

Thao Nguyen
Vietnam

___ EXERCISE 5K _____

1. Write the correct regular and irregular past tense verbs in the
   blanks.
2. Put boxes around each ⌊ , and⌉ and ⌊ , but⌉ that joins two
   clauses. Circle the subject for each clause.

3. Put parentheses around 3 negative verbs.

4. How was Thao's trip different from the other paragraphs in this chapter?

II

_____

After I _____ in Washington, D.C., I _____ a taxi
       arrive   **take**

to the hotel that had been reserved for me by my sponsor. I _____ to
                                                have

walk from my hotel to a restaurant to eat. ＊ I did not _____ that
                                              like

task. The complexity of the city roads, the large number of vehicles, and

the frightening traffic lights made crossing the road a terrible thing for

me. I was very frightened by the cars because I _____ that they
                                            assume

would crash into me. Therefore, I was very worried about my life during

my first weeks in the United States. I did not _____ friends to
                                            have

contact in case I had an accident in Washington. ＊ I was very careful

whenever I had to cross streets. Unfortunately, that _____ that
                                            mean

I always had to wait a very long time before crossing. Because of my

experiences in Washington, I _____ that in the U.S.A., one
                                        decide

should own a car, and one should never walk anywhere!

Hailu Kenno
Ethiopia

___ EXERCISE 5L _____

1. Write the correct regular and irregular past tense verbs in the blanks. Remember, the root form of the verb is used with the negative.

2. Use ⌊ , but⌋ or ⌊ , so⌋ to join two clauses where you see the asterisks (＊). Circle the subject for each clause.

3. Write a title for the paragraph.

4. What frightened Hailu?

III

Leaving My Village

One windy and sunny summer morning, my father called me and my grandmother into his private room. He ＿＿＿＿＿＿＿ us that, like every eighteen-year-old in my village, I must go to France. The following day, my father summoned all the village elders, and he ＿＿＿＿＿＿＿ to them about my departure. The morning of my departure, my father slaughtered a white cock, whose blood would protect me during my trip. Then he broke three cola nuts. Next to him stood my grandmother, who was very concerned about the trip. She spit on my head and ＿＿＿＿＿＿＿ me a bracelet that had belonged to her father before he died. This bracelet was a token for me to remember her by. At ten o'clock the wagon was ready, and I ＿＿＿＿＿＿＿ beside the driver. Immediately, my father started pouring holy water behind the horses, and he said, "I pray you, God, bless him." He continued until we drove off. I waved my left hand because, according to our custom, a man does not wave his right hand while he is leaving to go abroad. Thus, I ＿＿＿＿＿＿＿ my native village with great ceremony.

VERBS: give   leave   sit   speak   tell

Issaka Sarr
Mali

___ EXERCISE 5M _____

1. Write the correct irregular past tense verb in the blanks. Use each verb on the list only once.

2. Put parentheses around 5 prepositional phrases in the paragraph.

3. What do you remember about the paragraph?

4. What questions could you ask Issaka about this paragraph?

Write a paragraph about how you felt when you began a long trip. Use connectors, and use some regular and irregular past tense verbs. Use the chart below to plan your paragraph. Try to use some adjectives of feeling in your paragraph.

How I Felt When I Began a Long Trip

I felt _____ because _____

For example, _____

Then I felt _____ because _____

For example, _____

After that, I felt _____ because _____

_____

For example, _____

I also felt _____ because _____

For example, _____

_____

When you have finished writing your paragraph, exchange paragraphs with a classmate:

    A. Read that paragraph.

    B. Underline the regular and irregular past tense verbs.

    C. Circle the connectors.

    D. Put boxes around the ⌐, and⌐, ⌐, but⌐, or ⌐, so⌐ that joins two clauses.

Are there any questions you could ask your classmate about the paragraph?

—— WRITING ASSIGNMENT ————————————

Study the graph on page 125. Then write a paragraph that describes the chart. Use some of the sentences at the top of page 125 to write the paragraph.

According to the Institute of International Education, . . .

For example, more than (X) percent of international graduate student engineers in U.S. universities . . .

Moreover, (X) percent . . ., and (X) percent . . .

Some international graduate student engineers (X percent). . .

I think that there are so many international graduate student engineers at U.S. universities because . . .

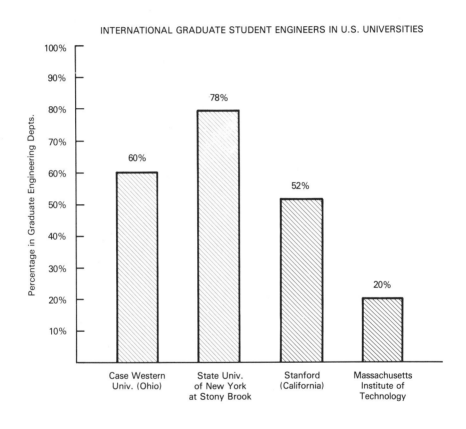

INTERNATIONAL GRADUATE STUDENT ENGINEERS IN U.S. UNIVERSITIES

Percentage in Graduate Engineering Depts.

- Case Western Univ. (Ohio): 60%
- State Univ. of New York at Stony Brook: 78%
- Stanford (California): 52%
- Massachusetts Institute of Technology: 20%

Friends are too many when you count them, but they are too few when you need them.

translated by
Adel Salameh
Iran

Read the paragraphs below. Then do the exercises that follow.

I

Welcome to the United States!

My uncle and his family were waiting for my wife and me when our plane _____ in San Francisco. We _____ very tired and dirty from our long trip. * My uncle made us feel happy. He greeted us warmly. * He helped us with our luggage. Our English was very poor. * My uncle _____ us. He took us to his car. * He _____ us to his home. During the drive, he showed us the Golden Gate Bridge and other famous sights. When we _____ at his home, we relieved our fatigue by taking long baths and sleeping. My wife _____ that she did not want to leave my uncle's home!

VERBS: arrive   drive   feel   help   land   say

Jun-Chul Shin
Korea

_____ EXERCISE 5N _____

1. Write the correct regular and irregular past tense verbs in the blanks. Use each verb on the list only once.
2. Write [, and] or [, but] to join two clauses where you see the asterisks (*).
3. Circle 5 possessive adjectives in the paragraph.
4. Why was Shin's arrival in the United States a pleasant experience?

II

My Anxious Feelings

When the plane landed in Los Angeles, I was very anxious. I had to face a new situation. * I did not know how to predict it. First, I had to stay with my uncle. * I had not met him before. I did not know whether he was a kind or a fierce man. * I did not know what his wife and children thought about me. A lot of questions came to my mind. In addition, my uncle and his family were Chinese, but I spoke Thai. I spoke Chinese just a little, but I could not communicate with his family because the Chinese I spoke was different from the Chinese my uncle's family spoke. Finally, this was the first time I had been away from my parents, and I had to decide everything by myself. That thought made me feel afraid. Therefore, as my plane landed, I was very anxious.

Suttinun Chivakunakorn
Thailand

___ EXERCISE 50 _____

1. Write [. and], [. but], or [. so] to join two clauses where you see the asterisks (∗).

2. Underline 4 negative verbs.

3. Why was Suttinun anxious about her arrival?

4. What questions did she have about her uncle's family?

_____

III

_____

I was so tired when I arrived in Portland after fourteen hours on airplanes, but that was just the beginning of my troubles. First, I hoped that my friend would meet me at the airport because I _____
                                                                    (negative) **know**

anything about the United States. I _____ how to leave the
                                     (negative) **understand**

airport. I _____ what to do next. Where was my luggage? I
           (negative) **know**

followed the crowd, and I finally found my bags. Then I discovered that it was raining outside, and it was cold. I _____ warm clothes,
                                                                (negative) **have**

and I _____ where my friend lived. Finally, a kind gentleman
      (negative) remember

showed me how to use the telephone book and the pay telephone, and at about midnight I was able to talk with my friend.

Chia-Chieh Chen
Taiwan (R.O.C.)

1. Write the correct negative past tense verbs in the blanks.
2. Put parentheses around 4 connectors in the paragraph.
3. Write a title for this paragraph.
4. What feelings do you think Chia-Chieh had when he arrived?

WRITING ASSIGNMENT

New Horizons Travel

2601 S. Lemay
Ft. Collins, CO 80525
(303) 223-7400

186 East 29th Street
Loveland, CO 80537
(303) 663-0663

```
SALES PERSON: 08                ITINERARY                      DATE: 08 AUG 85
CUSTOMER NBR: 000000                      YROPJT               PAGE:  1

                                                     INVOICE DUE UPON PRESENTATION
                                                     UNLESS PRIOR ARRANGEMENTS HAVE
                                                     BEEN MADE.
                                                     PLEASE RECONFIRM FLIGHTS


FOR:  Mario Ortega


10 OCT 85  -  THURSDAY
   AIR   LV DENVER                915AM   MEXICANA     FLT:919   COACH CLASS
         AR MEXICO CITY           305PM   2-STOPS
   AIR   LV MEXICO CITY           500PM   AEROLINEAS   FLT:385   COACH CLASS
         AR LIMA         PE      1125PM   NON-STOP     DINNER

31 OCT 85  -  THURSDAY
   AIR   LV LIMA         PE       145AM   VARIG        FLT:832   COACH CLASS
         AR LOS ANGELES           810AM   NON-STOP     DINNER
   AIR   LV LOS ANGELES          1100AM   UNITED       FLT:320   COACH CLASS
         AR DENVER                204PM   NON-STOP     LUNCH

      HAVE A NICE TRIP
      THANK YOU FOR CALLING NEW HORIZONS TRAVEL
      A 10.00 DOLLAR NON-REFUNDABLE FEE WILL APPLY ON
      ANY FULLY UNUSED TICKETS
```

Look at the flight schedule above. It shows Mario's trip to his home in Peru. Write a paragraph about his trip. Use past tense verbs and appropriate connectors in your paragraph. Answer some of the following questions:

Where did Mario begin his trip?

What airlines did Mario fly?

When did he leave?

Where did he go first?

How long did his first flight take?

How long did he wait at his first stop?

When did his next flight leave?

When did he arrive in Lima, Peru?

How long did his trip take?

What feelings do you think that Mario had when he arrived?

  ___ **INTERVIEW**

Ask a person NOT in your class to describe a long trip he or she took. Ask some of these questions:

Where did you go?

How long did you travel?

Did you have to change planes? Where?

Did you have any problems with the plane?

What other difficulties did you have?

What problems did you solve? How?

What feelings did you have when you arrived? Why?

Write a paragraph about your friend's trip. Use the correct subject and object pronouns. Exchange paragraphs with a classmate:

A. Read the paragraph.

B. Underline the regular and irregular past tense verbs.

C. Put parentheses around the connectors in the paragraph.

D. Circle the adjectives of feeling in the paragraph.

> A camel led by a camel, and a man led by a woman cannot step aside from you.
>
> translated by
> *Mohamud Fahie*
> Somalia

My Last Day in My Country

My Happiest Childhood Memory

What I Did Yesterday

A Fear I Had When I Was a Child

An Accident I Remember

What I Do When I Am Sick

My Favorite Children's Story

WRITING PROJECTS

Individual Project

On a world map, trace your long trip. Indicate the number of miles (or kilometers) between stops on the trip. Write the time each part of the trip took, and mark the places you stopped. Then write several paragraphs about your long trip. Use some of the topics below:

The First Part of My Trip

What I Ate During My Trip

A City Where My Plane Landed

The Best Part of My Trip

A Person I Met on My Trip

The Worst Part of My Trip

The Plane I Travelled On

My Feelings During My Trip

Put your paragraphs into a booklet. Decorate the booklet with maps, with postcards from the cities you visited, and with photographs. Display the booklet in your class, and invite students from other classes to view it.

Group Project

Make a booklet advising students travelling abroad about the necessary arrangements they need to make. Use a check list for students like the one below to plan your project. Have each student in the class write about such arrangements in their own countries. Interview several students NOT in your class about arrangements that need to be made in other countries. Illustrate the booklet with the necessary forms and diagrams that will help students prepare for study abroad. Present the booklet to the foreign student advisor to help him or her counsel study-abroad students.

Checklist for Students Travelling Abroad

3 months before the departure date:
go to the embassy _____
get visa _____
????????? _____

2 months before the departure date:
get papers _____
get academic transcripts _____
????????? _____

1 month before the departure date:
????????? _____
????????? _____

2 weeks before the departure date:
????????? _____
????????? _____

1 week before the departure date:
????????? _____
????????? _____

Six

First Impressions,
First Problems

The Airport

When I arrived at John F. Kennedy Airport in New York, I was really surprised because it was so big. First, the airport is divided into many small airports, one for each airline (like TWA and United and American Airlines). The gates for all the flights are very extensive, but the information about flights is hung on the walls, so I did not become lost. When I finally found where to pick up my luggage, I went outside the airport because I had to travel to another airport to catch my next plane. I saw many parking lots, high buildings, and very wide roads, and I saw a lot of vans that transport people and their luggage from airport to airport. Above me, many planes were taking off and landing. There were so many that I couldn't count them; if I had been in my country, I would have said that they were birds, not planes. The noise from all these planes was unbelievable, but I thought it was wonderful.

Safouen Ben Brahim
Tunisia

ADJECTIVES AND ADVERBS*

adjective + noun (WHAT KIND?)	verb + adverb (HOW?)
a *long* street	I walked *slowly*.
an *ugly* picture	He reads *easily*.
the *quiet* child	You explain *clearly*.
the *large* city	We left *quickly*.
beautiful flowers	They dance *gracefully*.
available food	
my *terrible* examinations	
his *annual* vacation	

Adjective endings				Adverb Ending	
-ful	(help*ful*)	-able	(lov*able*)	-ly	quiet*ly*
-ous	(danger*ous*)	-al	(medic*al*)		
-ive	(informat*ive*)	-le	(terrib*le*)		
-less	(help*less*)	-ing	(interest*ing*)*		
		-ed	(frighten*ed*)*		

NOTE: Sometimes verbs in English are used as adjectives.

Adjective	Adverb
He is a *careful* driver.	He drives *carefully*.
They are *quick* learners.	They learn *quickly*.

Exceptions

He is a *FAST* runner.　　　He runs *FAST*.

They ate *HARD* candy.　　　They worked *HARD*.

Verb + Adverb + Adjective

She	is	real*ly*	**quiet**.
Faizah	was	especial*ly*	surpris*ed*.
Masako	seems	**very**	tir*ed*.

Golden-Thread Clothes

Desire not golden-thread clothes.
Rather, enjoy your youth.
Good flowers are worth picking,
so go ahead and pick.
Don't wait until the flowers are gone,
and you can only pick the stem.

translated by
Prayat Laopropassone
Thailand

—— EXERCISE 6A ——

Look at the adjectives below. Cross out the adjectives that do not fit with the nouns.

green		old	
blond		thick	
long		yellow	
gray	} hair	tall	} book
curly		fast	
old		good	
straight		interesting	

---

*See Appendix B for spelling rules, and Appendix C for a list of some adjectives and adverbs.

beautiful		black	
strong		lazy	
tall		long	
slow	} coffee	good	} student
bitter		angry	
hot		expensive	
good		excellent	
new		fat	
wood		sad	
fat		nice	
metal	} table	noisy	} baby
broken		wood	
crying		hungry	
long		short	

_____ EXERCISE 6B _____

Write adjectives in the blanks that describe the nouns below.

_____

_____

_____ school

_____

_____

_____

_____ picture

_____

_____

_____

_____ car

_____

_____

_____

_____ coat

_____

A *Pleasant* Surpise

When I first came to the U.S., the street where I lived surprised me because it was [very] clean and nice. On my first night in Santa Barbara, I went for a long walk around the neighborhood, and I did not see a single piece of paper or even a small piece of trash on the quiet street. In front of almost every house there were [many] beautiful flowers, and their smell, combined with the fresh air, followed me everywhere I went. I felt like I was in the country. Soft music escaped pleasantly from the house at the end of the street, so the sound of the darkness was like an endless song. In the large city where I grew up, there was an ugly pile of trash every two or three blocks. I could smell the garbage from my doorstep, and I could hear noisy car engines and motorcycles all day and all night. My neighbors argued [loudly] and [endlessly]. Because I expected the U.S. to be like my own country, I was [very] surprised when I saw the <u>elegant</u> street in my <u>new</u> neighborhood.

Mai Anh Tran
Vietnam

Read the paragraphs on the following pages. Then do the exercises that follow.

I

Strange Things

Moving from my country to continue my graduate study in the United States was a good chance for me. But when I first came to the U.S., I was very unhappy because I encountered many strange things. The strange people were especially surprising. I found that nobody spoke my language, and everybody wore funny clothes. So people for me were as different as the fingers on my hand. Another strange thing was the terrible food. For example, most American food contains at least a derivative of pork, but pork is forbidden by my religion. The third strange thing was the changeable weather. A single day could have a warm morning, a cold afternoon, and a thunderstorm! I was not used to living in such a changeable climate and different living conditions, so I was unhappy.

Khalid Al-Sawaf
Saudi Arabia

—— EXERCISE 6C ——————————————

1. Underline at least 5 adjectives in the paragraph.
2. Circle 2 adverbs.
3. Put boxes around the ,and , ,but , or , so that joins two clauses.
4. What questions could you ask Khalid about this paragraph? What other paragraphs could Khalid write?

II

No Kissing!

It was the first day of my arrival in the U.S. On that day, I

_____ very excited, and I _____ to express that to all my

friends. Traditionally, in my country, when a man meets another man he

has not seen for a long time, he expresses his good fortune toward him.

They shake hands vigorously, and they kiss each other. Their true

feelings appear at that moment. Therefore, on the university campus,

when I _____ my friend, I pulled him toward me in order to kiss

him. I was surprised because he refused to do so. He _____

quickly, "Oh, my dear friend, it is not a good idea. Everyone will think we

are gay!" I _____ him angrily, saying, "What do you mean? We

do this back home. It is a very valuable thing, is it not?" Then he

_____ the problem to me. After that, I swore that I would never,

never kiss a man in the U.S.!

VERBS: answer   explain   feel   say   see   want

Qassen Al-Jalut
Iraq

___ EXERCISE 6D _____

1. Write the correct past tense verbs in the blanks. Use each verb on the list only once.
2. Underline 4 adjectives in the paragraph.
3. Circle at least 5 adverbs in the paragraph.
4. Why was Qassen so surprised?

> If you want to have an average living,
> you must have the habit of saving.
> If you want to be very rich,
> you must be very lucky.
>
> translated by
> *Man-Chiu Lu*
> Malaysia

Read the paragraphs below and on the following pages. Then do the exercises that follow.

I

Traffic

One of the most important things that surprised me in the U.S.A. is the attention paid to traffic safety. The government _____ the streets and highways carefully, so they _____ usually wide and divided. On both sides of the wide streets, there are large traffic signs which control the flow of heavy traffic on the roads. The signs with the speed limits and the traffic rules _____ fluorescent paint, so they can be seen easily at night. In addition, the citizens participate in traffic safety by obeying the laws. They always _____ when the signs say stop, and they are careful at every moment. They do not park their cars wherever they want, and they do not throw trash in the streets. Besides that, the policemen _____ to fix stalled cars, so the flow of traffic continues perfectly. All of these arrangements gave me a nice picture about the traffic in the U.S.A.

VERBS: be   have   help   plan   stop

Ivan Hernandez
Venezuela

_____ EXERCISE 6E _____

1. Write the correct present tense verbs in the blanks. Use each verb on the list only once.
2. Underline at least 5 adjectives. Circle 4 adverbs.
3. Why is the title of this paragraph "Traffic"?
4. What do you remember about the paragraph?

II
Happiness

During my first weeks in the U.S., I _____ happiness. Before I _____ to the U.S., I was on the staff of a fabric company, and I worked in a busy office. It seemed that I was on a battlefield. Of course, in those days, I did not notice the terrible environment because I was used to the atmosphere. Fortunately, I did not know there was a happy and gentle town like Lawrence, Kansas. When I arrived in Lawrence, I was very surprised at the beauty of the town, the quiet atmosphere, and the kindness of the people. I had had some impressions about America, and they _____ negative. However, the happiness that I found in Lawrence _____ my negative impressions. I was charmed by the town and the people, and I was really glad that I had made a good decision about the city where I would study in America. My great happiness, however, was that I found a beautiful and peaceful town which was quite different from my office. I love my town in Japan, and I also love my new hometown in America.

VERBS: be   change   come   find

Kimimasa Abe
Japan

_____ EXERCISE 6F _____

1. Write the correct past tense verbs in the blanks. Use each verb on the list only once.
2. Underline at least 8 adjectives in the paragraph, and circle 3 adverbs.
3. What surprised Kimimasa?
4. Why is he happy?

Dogs are treated differently in the United States than in my home country, Saudi Arabia. In my country, people treat dogs the same as they treat any animal. They do not like dogs. * Dogs are not allowed to enter houses. If a large number of dogs gather together in a neighborhood, people try to get rid of them. Dogs usually live around garbage areas. * People think they are dirty animals. If, by any chance, a dog touches a person's clothes, that person needs to wash his clothes immediately. But in the U.S., the situation is completely different. Here, dogs are considered as pets. People like them, and they are very proud of their dogs. Dogs live in houses with people. They sit on the sofas or even on the beds. They have special food, special clothes, and even special hospitals! Moreover, in the U.S., I have seen some people kiss their dogs. It was really a shock for me!

Mahamoud Wali
Saudi Arabia

___ EXERCISE 6G _____

1. Underline 3 adjectives, and circle 4 adverbs in the paragraph.
2. Join two clauses where you see the asterisk (*) with `, and` or `, so` .
3. Write a title for the paragraph.
4. Why was Mahamoud shocked?

> If water could go uphill, the frog would sing, too.
>
> translated by
> *Keyvan Karbassiyon*
> Iran

___ WRITING ASSIGNMENT _____

Write a paragraph about a surprising problem you encountered in a new place or a new situation. Describe how you solved the problem. Use adjectives to describe the situation and your feelings. Answer some of the questions below to plan the paragraph.

What was the problem?

What did you expect?

What was different from your expectations?

What was similar to your expectations?

What did you discover?

Why were you surprised?

How did you feel about the problem? Happy? Anxious? Angry? Sad? Frustrated? WHY?

What did you do first?

Then what did you do?

Finally, what happened?

Exchange paragraphs with a classmate. Read the paragraph.

    A. Underline the adjectives, and circle the adverbs.

    B. Put parentheses around the prepositional phrases.

    C. Do you have any questions about your classmate's paragraph?

    D. What other paragraphs could your classmate write?

SPECIAL VERBS

I *see* [*saw*] the airplane flying overhead.   (Briefly)

I *look at* [*looked at*] my visa.   (Carefully)

       *   *   *   *   *

I *hear* [*heard*] the airplane flying overhead.   (Briefly)

I *listen to* [*listened to*] the stereo.   (Carefully)

       *   *   *   *   *

They *say that* [*said that*] they were homesick.

They *tell* (me, my friend) *that* [*told* (me, my friend) *that*] they were homesick.

Mosquitos!

    I HEARD a lot of stories about the U.S. back in my country, Nigeria. One person SAID THAT there were no mosquitos or insects in the United States because of the cold climate. However, five days after my arrival in Macomb, Illinois, I SAW mosquitos outside our living room door. I was saying goodbye to some visitors when I first SAW the mosquitos. Then I LOOKED AT my son, and I SAW a mosquito on his arm. I grabbed his arm, and I killed the mosquito. Suddenly I <u>HEARD</u> my little daughter cry because another mosquito had bitten her. I rushed to her and killed the mosquito, and blood gushed out on my palms. My daughter's hand was a bit swollen the following day. So I <u>TOLD</u> my husband <u>THAT</u> it was not true that there were not mosquitos in the U.S., and I wondered why I had <u>LISTENED TO</u> the stories in Nigeria.

Margaret A. Obaja
Nigeria

Read the paragraphs below and on the next page. Then do the exercises that follow.

I

Homesickness

When I first saw my apartment in the U.S., I cried. I married my husband one week before we came here. * I left my wonderful family for the first time. Every day my husband went to the university. * I stayed in the apartment. I cleaned the room and our clothes. * Then I thought about my family and my good friends. I tried to listen to the radio. * I could not understand the language. I watched television. * I did not understand. Then I cried. * I spent many hours looking at beautiful photographs of my family. For two months I stayed in that terrible apartment. I did not go to the university or to the supermarket. I did not have any friends. I stayed in my apartment. * I cried when I remembered my friends.

Hussa Al-Hitmi
Qatar

__ EXERCISE 6H __

1. Underline the "special verbs": <u>see,</u> <u>listen to,</u> <u>watch,</u> <u>look at.</u>
2. Circle at least 2 adjectives in the paragraph.
3. Join two clauses where you see the asterisks (*) with [, and] or [, but] .
4. Why was Hussa so unhappy? What advice could you give her to make her experience better?

II
Machines

One thing that really amazed me when I first _____ in the United States was the large number of things one can get from coin-operated machines. During my first hours in the United States, I was able to buy many things without making contact with a human being. All I _____ was a few coins in my hand. For example, I saw machines all around the airport. I _____ a can of Coke, a candy bar, and a pack of gum because I was very hungry. Later, at my hotel, I saw more machines, so I bought some chips and a newspaper, and I put coins in the television to watch a movie. When I told my friends about my unusual experiences, they laughed. Then they _____ me machines that sold postage stamps and air letters, even when the post office _____ closed. For entertainment, I _____ I could use coins to play video games or listen to the music of my choice on juke boxes in restaurants. Now, when I put coins into a machine to do my laundry, I also buy cigarettes and coffee from machines in the laundromat. I never go anywhere without a handful of coins!

VERBS:　　arrive　　be　　buy　　find　　need　　show

Leung Lai
Singapore

_____ EXERCISE 6l _____

1. Write the past tense verbs in the blanks. Use each verb on the list only once.
2. Underline the "special verbs"; <u>see</u>, <u>listen to</u>, <u>tell</u>.
3. Circle 2 adjectives and 2 adverbs in the paragraph.
4. What do you remember about the paragraph?

> Nothing can cool off your itches like your own fingernails.
>
> translated by
> *Adel Salamah*
> Iran

 **INTERVIEW**

Interview someone NOT in your class about:

    A. his or her first impression of a new situation or a new place

OR

    B. his or her most surprising problem in a new situation or a new place.

Ask some of the questions on pages 140–141 to help plan the paragraph. In the paragraph, use such expressions as:

    he said that . . .

    she told me that . . .

Use adjectives and adverbs in the paragraph. In some sentences, use ⌐, and⌐ , ⌐, but⌐ , *or* ⌐, so⌐ *to join two clauses.*

Exchange paragraphs with a classmate. Read the paragraph.

    A. Underline the special verbs: <u>say</u>, <u>tell</u>.

    B. Circle the adjectives and the adverbs.

    C. Put boxes around two clauses that are joined by ⌐, and⌐ , ⌐, but⌐ , or ⌐, so⌐ .

    D. What questions could you ask your classmate about the paragraph?

SPECIAL ADVERBS: TOO AND VERY

> The weather was **very** cold, but I could still go outside.
> (possible but difficult)
>
> The weather was **too** cold, so I could *not* go outside.
> (negative, impossible)

Culture Shock

When a person travels from his home country to another one, he will somtimes feel VERY uncomfortable. This is called "culture shock." One thing that shocked me when I came to the States was the "tip" or "tax." For example, I entered the U.S. in San Francisco, and I spent one night in a hotel that cost $35 per night. The next morning I prepared $35 to pay my bill. I was very surprised when the clerk asked for a little more than $35. I thought he was making me pay <u>TOO</u> much. However, he told me that the additional money was for tax. He also said that I must leave a 10%–15% tip. Thus I paid more than I was prepared to pay. I have learned that most merchandise in the U.S. is taxed. Even when I buy food at the market, the clerk charges about 5% of the total receipt. Also, whenever I go to a restaurant, I leave a tip at my place for 15% of the bill. Although there are no tips or taxes in China, I am learning about the U.S. culture.

Jin Lu
China (P.R.C.)

Read the paragraphs below and on the following pages. Then do the exercises that follow.

I

Housing

When I left Korea for my first trip abroad, I expected many things. But I did not know that finding an apartment would be so frustrating. When I arrived, my friend took me to the university housing office. The secretary said, "It's very difficult to give you university housing at this moment— maybe in three months." I felt very anxious, but my friend helped me look in the newspaper "want ads." We went to look at two or three apartments, but there was a problem. <u>I had to sign a contract for a year</u>. Therefore, I would not be able to move to university housing in three months. My friends tried to encourage me, but I could not think about anything. <u>I was very worried about the problem</u>. I was living in a hotel, and I was spending too much money. <u>Finally, I found an apartment at Prospect Plaza</u>. <u>The rooms in the apartment were very clean</u>. The manager gave me a checklist about the apartment, and he told me to check any problems in the apartment. Then I signed a three-month contract, and my friend helped me move my luggage into the apartment.

Jong-Hub Park
Korea

1. Underline the special adverbs: <u>too</u> and <u>very</u>. What does each mean in the paragraph?
2. Make the underlined sentences negative.
3. Put boxes around the [, and] or [, but] that joins two clauses.
4. Why was finding an apartment frustrating for Park?

II

Cooking

Probably the worst experience I _____ during my life in the U.S. was in the kitchen: cooking, washing dishes, shopping, etc. Of course, I first experienced life in restaurants, but after only two weeks I _____ so broke that I did not want to think more about eating in restaurants. Besides the fact that the restaurants cost too much, I was never able to understand the menus, unless they came with some nice pictures. Therefore, I _____ to start my kitchen "studies." At the beginning, I _____ really humiliated since I was still thinking like I did at home. I thought that the kitchen was the kind of job only for women. What a silly idea! Then I was very ashamed of myself for not being able to do the simple kitchen work. I still remember my first dinner, if it could be called dinner. It was boiled, salted rice with hard chicken. I _____ it all because I was really hungry, and also I did not want to demonstrate my incompetence to my roommate.

VERBS: be   decide   eat   feel   have

Hervé John Raymond
Haiti

1. Write the correct past tense verbs in the blanks. Use each verb on the list only once.
2. Underline the special adverbs: <u>too</u> and <u>very</u>. What does each mean in the paragraph?

3. Circle three verbs + adjectives of feeling in the paragraph.

4. Why did Hervé feel humiliated?

III

Distressing Complexities

I was very distressed by the complexity of daily life in the first two months after I arrived in the U.S. For example, the complex procedures to see a doctor are very different from those in my country. In the U.S., I found that I could not go to see a doctor immediately if I felt sick because I needed to make an appointment first. I always had to wait a few days to get into his schedule. For example, two weeks after I arrived, I called a doctor's office to make an appointment for a fungus infection on my foot. The nurse told me that the schedule was full. Two days later the infection was worse, and it hurt terribly. After the doctor made his diagnosis, he gave me a prescription. However, I needed to go to the pharmacy to fill it instead of getting the medicine directly from the doctor. Finally, when I paid the doctor's bill, the nurse asked me if I had insurance. We do not think of medical insurance when we go to the doctor in my country, but we certainly must in the U.S. because without insurance, medical expenses are too great. In my country, this entire experience would only have taken one day, but in the U.S. it took more than two weeks to solve the problem of my infected foot.

Chia-Chu Dorland
Taiwan (R.O.C.)

___ EXERCISE 6L _____

1. Underline the special adverbs: <u>too</u> and <u>very</u>. What does each mean in the paragraph?

2. Circle at least two adjectives and two adverbs.

3. Put parentheses around the pronouns in the paragraph. Identify the subject pronouns (S) and the object pronouns (O).

4. What did Chia-Chu do before she saw the doctor?

> Learning is like a boat going upstream:
> if one does not row hard enough,
> the boat will definitely go down the stream.
>
> translated by
> *Man-Chiu Lu*
> Malaysia

You have just arrived in the U.S., and you are looking for an apartment. Read the newspaper "want ads" below. Then write a paragraph about looking for an apartment. Answer some of the questions below to help plan the paragraph. Use adjectives and adverbs in your paragraph. Use time connectors and present tense verbs.

708 Rentals to share

SHARE newly remodeled 2-bdrm apt with male. Fully furnished except bdrm, $150/month, ½ utilities. 224-9214.

SHARE QUIET 3 bdrm, 1 mile CSU, fenced, laundry, $175 plus ⅓ utilities. 493-3180 after 5pm

SHARE 2 bdrm apt., fireplace, cheap utilities, new washer/dryer! $207.50/deposit. 224-5525.

TO SHARE 3 bdrm newer house, close to CSU, fireplace, gas grill, fenced yard, nice area, $150/month, 224-4340/484-6291

TO SHARE 4-bdrm house. $155/month. plus utilities. Clean and responsible persons need only inquire. Rob 482-2956.

710 Rooms to rent

ABDICATE HIGH RENT. Private room, cozy. 510 S Howes. $100 per mo 1-669-6754 collect.

AVAILABLE IN home, Jan. 15. Near Fashion Mall and bus routes. Washer/dryer, quiet. $165 plus utilities. 223-0097.

FURNISHED sleeping room $112/mo utilities paid. Refrigerator space available. 221-5888
MAIL CREEK PROPERITES

ROOM FOR NON-SMOKER Kitchen privleges. $175 Plus deposit. 482-1285

ROOMY SUITE. Female, non-smoker, fireplace, rent for horse care. $235/$195. 493-8220.

712 Furnished apartments

A BASEMENT 2 BDRM, very clean, close to CSU, $275. Bunton Realty, 221-1600 or 221-3843.

ACROSS FROM NEW HOLIDAY INN! Studios, 1 and 2 bdrms, all utilities paid. $245, $300, $360
304 W Prospect, 482-9513

A QUIET 2 BDRM BASEMENT, near the malls. Adults only. Many extras. Call 221-1788.

AVAILABLE. 2 bdrm, very clean, near Moby Gym, pet ok, $350. Bunton Realty, 221-1600 or 221-3843.

BEST DEALS in town 1-bdrm $225 2/3 bills paid garage. Renter's Guide 484-1380 Fee C-1

BUFFET with kitchenette, $185/month includes utilities. Horsetooth area. 226-2934

CAMBRIDGE HOUSE Apts. has 2 bdrm apts. with free cable tv, indoor pool and clubhouse. Right across from CSU, 1113 W. Plum. 484-7756.

CLEAN 1-bdrm, available , n 1. $275 Plus utilities. No pets. 915 James Court. 1-499-5709

WON'T LAST. Studio and 2 bdrm apartments, close to CSU. Pool, furnished or unfurnished. $225-$395. 775 W. Lake, call Russ. 484-1446 1-5 PM or Foxfire Property Management, 224-9207, No Fee.

KITCHENETTES, special winter rates. TV, phone, laundry, weekly, monthly. Plainsman Motel, 482-9744, 1310 N. College.

LARGE BRIGHT 1 bdrm basement apt. Share kitchen with one other. City Park area. $200, share utilities. 493-4543.

LARGE 1 BDRM, all utilities paid except electric, next to campus, $300 a month. 224-3616.

NICE 1-bdrm close to CSU. $275. 919 James Court. Anderson CO 484-5115

ONE-EXTRA large bdrm in 4-plex. Heat/water/sewer/trash paid, no pets. $300. Anderson Company 484-5115

QUIET 2 BDRM basement apartment, 1 block from campus, no smokers, or pets $250 a month plus utilities. Available Feb. 1. Call 493-9031.

SCOTCH PINES EAST

Furnished studio, all appliances plus washer/dryer, fireplace, outdoor pool, clubhouse, tennis courts, adult area, 3 or 6 month lease, $300 plus utilities. 915 East Drake Road, 223-4038

HEATHERIDGE! 2 bdrm, 1½ baths, laundry, amenities. No pets. $395. Mountain-N-Plains, 221-2361, 8-5. Sat. 9-12. No Fee.

HEAT PAID, 1-bdrm. 610 Stover, No 3. Cat OK. Courtyard, $260. 221-0763; 493-5290 after 5pm

Finding an Apartment

Information I need to know *before* I begin looking:

_____

_____

_____

Questions I need to ask the apartment manager:

_____

_____

_____

What kind of apartment I need:

_____

_____

_____

 **INTERVIEW**

Ask a friend NOT in your class about his or her needs for an apartment. Write a "want ad" for a newspaper that describes that apartment. Make the "want ad" brief, but make it complete and clear. Include all the necessary information.

The current will take any shrimp that is not awake.

translated by
Douglas Chang
Ecuador

PRESENT CONTINUOUS VERBS (RIGHT NOW)*

TO BE + VERB + -ING

I *am cooking* dinner. (right now)

He *is watching* television. (right now)

She *is listening* to the radio. (right now)

It *is snowing*. (right now)

You *are talking* on the telephone. (right now)

We *are looking* at an apartment. (right now)

They *are running*. (right now)

*See the inside front cover of this book for spelling rules.

Adjustments

Last week, my husband Armando and I arrived in Mexico City. This week I AM ADJUSTING to my new life, but I AM HAVING some problems. First, I do not know the city, so I must depend on Armando's friends to help me. I was very independent when I lived in the U.S., so this is difficult for me. Second, I AM not WORKING because we will be moving to Aguascalientes in two months. Therefore, I AM SPENDING my time reading, cooking, and washing and ironing Armando's shirts. Finally, we ARE LIVING with a family. The man IS WORKING in the same company as Armando. The people are very nice, but the situation does have some disadvantages. So although we are not established in a normal way of life, we will soon move to a new town and our own apartment.

Susan Yamine Valencia
United States

Read the paragraphs below and on the following pages. Then do the exercises that follow.

I

Arrival in Jeddah

Jeddah is not what I expected. I was surprised, for example, that English is the official business language, so I _____

be + not + have

trouble with my day-to-day activities. I _____ in

be + live

a nice two-bedroom home on the company compound. The company

_____ excellent support facilities like a gymnasium,

be + provide

scuba diving, and tennis courts. I _____ a university

be + take

course in computer science and a class in Arabic, so I am very busy.

Besides my life in the compound, there is quite a lot to do in the city itself.

Tonight I _____ to see one of the theater groups

be + go

perform, and I have also been to the opera and to the square dance club.
In short, I _____ life here to be quite enjoyable.
be + find

Doug Ellis
United States

___ EXERCISE 6M _____

1. Write the correct present continuous verb in the blanks.
2. Put boxes around the [, and] or [, so] that joins two clauses.
3. Put parentheses around 4 adjectives and 1 adverb in the paragraph.
4. Why was Jeddah a surprise for Doug?

II

Cusco's Street Sounds

One of the most surprising things about Cusco, Peru is the street
sounds. Right now I _____ to men calling for bottles,
be + listen

and the scissor sharpeners with their continual special call. Dozens of
horns _____, and the cars are very noisy. I don't
be + honk

think they have any mufflers at all. The street vendors

_____ to the passersby, and the beggars
be + shout

_____ to the tourists. Because it is a weekend,
be + call

there is also music in the street, and people _____
be + dance

to celebrate a feast day. All of those sounds _____
be + blend

together into a unique concert, and I am glad that I am here to hear it.

Selma Myers
United States

_____ EXERCISE 6N _____

1. Write the correct present continuous verbs in the blanks.
2. Put boxes around [, and / that joins two clauses.
3. Put parentheses around 5 prepositional phrases.
4. What noises does Selma hear in Cusco?

III

Los Baños, Laguna in the Philippines has impressed me with

its tropical climate. Green is everywhere: leaves, vines, bushes. I

_____ confused by the disorder, and I am some-
    be + feel

times a little frightened by the abundant growth. The humidity and

the heat of the country are also a great change from the dry plains of

my home in the United States. I _____ stockings and
                    be + abandon

other unnecessary clothing, and I usually dress in thongs, a cotton

blouse, and a skirt. The frequent rain differs from the cold, chilling rain of

my hometown. Here, with 90 percent humidity in eighty-five degree air,

there is no shock to the body when slightly more concentrated mois-

ture falls in the form of rain. My skin _____ from
                be + benefit

the moisture. It _____ and even youthful. Now
        be + glow

that I _____ to the climate in Los Baños, I
    be + adjust

_____ more comfortable.
   be + feel

Ann Zimdahl
United States

_____ EXERCISE 6O _____

1. Write the correct present continuous verbs in the blanks.
2. Circle 5 adjectives and 2 adverbs in the paragraph.

3. Write a title for this paragraph.

4. How does the rain in Los Baños differ from rain in Ann's hometown?

___ WRITING ASSIGNMENT _____

Choose a classmate. Write a paragraph about that classmate. Describe what he or she is doing RIGHT NOW. Use present continuous verbs. Use adjectives and adverbs. Answer some of the questions below.

What is he or she wearing?

Is he or she sitting? Standing? Studying?

What is he or she doing? Now? Now? Now?

What is he or she thinking about?

Exchange paragraphs with that classmate. Read the paragraph.

A. Underline the present continuous verbs.

B. Circle the adjectives.

C. Put a box around the [, and] , [, but] , or [, so] that joins two clauses.

D. Is the description written by your classmate accurate? Discuss this point.

PAST CONTINUOUS VERBS (LAST WEEK, YESTERDAY)*

BE + VERB + -ING
I **was visiting** my friend. (yesterday)
He **was planning** his trip. (last week)
She **was having** some problems. (last month)
It **was raining** very hard. (last April)
You **were living** with your friend. (last year)
We **were walking** to the train station. (yesterday)
They **were working** together. (last Tuesday)
*See the inside front cover of this book for spelling rules.

___ EXERCISE 6P ___

Read the paragraph below. Write the correct past continuous verbs in the blanks.

Reverse Culture Shock

I experienced reverse culture shock when I _____
be + visit

Italy on holiday from Rumania last year. It was the day before

Christmas, and I was on my way to Italy. The previous week in Rumania

had been particularly bad. It was bitter cold, and only a few trolleys

_____ because of an energy problem. Crowds of people
be + run

_____ into the street. They _____
be + drift   **be + search**

for transportation. The day before I left for Italy, a big shipment of

oranges came from Turkey, and as I _____, I saw a
be + leave

line of frozen people that stretched for three city blocks. Everyone

_____ for Christmas oranges. The next night, as my bus
be + wait

_____ the border of Yugoslavia into Italy, the first
be + cross

little town was decorated with enough lights to support Bucharest for a

couple of days. Carts of fruit spilled out of store doorways into the night

air. I was surprised to see bananas and pineapples. All this fruit, and no

one _____ it! Great carcasses of meat hung from the
be + buy

ceiling of a brightly lit butcher shop. The Christmas lights densely lined the

streets, and there was food everywhere. But suddenly I was surprised to discover that I really wanted to go back to Bucharest where life was stark and simple.

Marian Aitches
United States

> No one feels the fire except the person who steps in it.
>
> translated by
> *Fawzi El-Nassir*
> Iraq

Read the paragraphs below. Then do the exercises that follow.

I

Competence and Incompetence

Life in the United States encourages people to become competent. I did not realize how important being useful and competent was for me until I went to Taiwan. When our plane landed, I decided to smile through all the experiences that we would have. However, because I did not know the Chinese language, I immediately began to have problems. First, our friend did not meet us at the airport. I tried to telephone him, but I could not get the telephone to work. A gentleman spoke to me in Mandarin Chinese. I did not understand him, so he took the number I had written, and he telephoned my friend. However, he obviously thought that I was not very intelligent. Then, as we _____ for our friend, I felt
be + waiting
useless. I was not competent in this new world, and so I had no worth. Later that evening, as we _____ along the streets to our
be + walk
new apartment, I started to cry. I _____ in the middle of
be + stand
the street, stating loudly (in English) that I wanted to go home!

Lois Thomas
United States

1. Write the correct past continuous verbs in the blanks.
2. Circle 6 negative verbs in the paragraph.
3. Why is the title of this paragraph "Competence and Incompetence"?
4. Why did Lois cry? Have you felt this way?

II

First Impressions of Mali

My first impression of Mali is that the people are wonderful. Right now, my husband and I _____ in a large private room

be + live

in a family home in Bamako. The family is very aware of our needs and our differences. Of course, they are amazed that we are incompetent at doing simple things, but they _____ us to learn. For

be + help

example, this morning I _____ wash clothes in a

be + learn

bucket and to use my left hand as a washboard. Yesterday I tried to pound millet with a mortar and pestle, and I watched the woman in the family as she _____ dried nuts. Shopping for food is

be + shell

another lesson I _____ today. Most fresh food is sold

be + practice

in open markets, and I must bargain in both French and Bambara. Fortunately, the Malians accept my feeble attempts to speak their language, and I _____ slowly _____

be +   improve

my French.

Linda Stratton
United States

1. Write the correct present AND past continuous verbs in the blanks. How do you know which tense to use?

2. Circle two adjectives in the paragraph.

3. Put parentheses around five prepositional phrases.

4. What is Linda learning in Bamako?

III

Impressions Upon Returning Home

After spending a year in France, my family and I returned to the
United States for a month's visit. We were surprised to find how different
and strange the United States had become. As we _____
                                               be + leave

the airport, we noticed how much bigger everything seemed. The cars,
the highways, and the potholes were huge! Life also seemed so much faster.
Everyone _____ somewhere, and no one looked very
               be + hurry

happy. We _____ too, trying to shop, to see the dentist
               be + hurry

and doctor, and to visit friends. For us, the most frustrating thing was
the lack of public transportation. We had to drive our car everywhere,
and American drivers are not as courteous as we had thought! Of course,
we enjoyed American beef, American ice cream, and especially iced tea,
but we were sad about the filthy roadsides, the graffiti, and the ever-
present television programs. As we _____ to France,
                                be + return

we all agreed that we would be much more tolerant of our life in Paris!

Ruth Doré
United States

--- EXERCISE 6S ---

1. Write the correct past continuous verbs in the blanks.

2. Circle the pronouns in the paragraph, and identify them as subject
   pronouns (S) or object pronouns (O).

3. How is this paragraph different from the previous two paragraphs?

4. What do you remember about the paragraph?

___ **WRITING ASSIGNMENT** _____

You are a student on a U.S. university campus, and you are surprised when you see the picture below in the university newspaper. Write a paragraph that describes the picture. Use present continuous verbs, and use adjectives and adverbs.

Bomar, a four-year-old, fifty-pound shepherd-husky dog, gets a ride from his owner, Jim Hoffman, a senior at Colorado State University. Hoffman said that Bomar enjoys riding this way and has done so for the past three years. The pair, traveling on Balsam Lane, were on their way to visit a friend. (*Photo courtesy of* The Fort Collins Coloradoan *newspaper*)

Exchange paragraphs with a classmate.

    A. Read the paragraph.

    B. Underline the present continuous verbs.

    C. Circle the adjectives.

    D. Put parentheses around the adverbs.

Rewrite your paragraph. Use past tense verbs instead of present continuous verbs.

____ EXERCISE 6T _____

Read the poem below. Underline the adjectives and circle the adverbs in the poem.

Lionrise

Glowing softly,
the giant yellow head
lifts itself from the cold ground.
The golden streamers
shimmer softly
and settle quietly into place.
Shading its face
with a fluffy orange paw
(which just happened to be drifting by)
it yawns discreetly,
closing lighted eyes
for only a moment,
enjoying one last sigh of darkness.
Flexing sleepy muscles
it climbs to its feet
and swishes its tail,
creating a small whirlwind
that gradually separates
into hundreds of individual breezes
that drift gently off
and disappear into the crisp morning air.
A brilliant eye
scans the blue savannah
and the crystal mountains
over which it must journey
before the day is over.
Beaming warmly down

on the awakening world,
it sets supple limbs in motion
and pads quietly off
toward the western horizon.

E. Shelley Reid
United States

___ **WRITING ASSIGNMENT** _____

*Translate a short poem from your language into English. Under-
line the adjectives and circle the adverbs in your translation.
Then write a paragraph that describes the problems you had
translating the poem. Use past tense regular and irregular
verbs, and use adjectives and adverbs in the paragraph.*

OTHER WRITING ASSIGNMENTS

How My First Impressions of Someone Were Right (or Wrong)

How My First Impressions of Something Were Right (or Wrong)

One Thing About My Country That a Foreign Visitor Might Find Surprising (or Strange, or Frightening)

How I Prepared Mentally for My Long Trip

WRITING PROJECTS

Individual Project

Translate several poems and sayings from your language. Make a booklet of these sayings. You might also include several children's stories from
your culture. Decorate the booklet with pictures and artwork. Present the
booklet to the children's section of the public library.

Group Project

Make a booklet with paragraphs about culture shock. Use the paragraphs written by class members, and interview other students about their
experiences with culture shock. Write those paragraphs, and include them
in the booklet. Illustrate the booklet with drawings and cartoons. Make copies of the booklet for the students who participated, and present a copy of
the booklet to the Office of International Services, the International Education Department, or the foreign student advisor for use in their orientations
and crosscultural classes.

Seven

Adjustments and Solutions

Adjustments

My life in college was not simple at first because I had to adjust to two new changes. My first adjustment was in my school life. The studies were different from those in high school, so I had to learn new ways of studying. For example, I could not rely on a summary that the teacher gave after each lesson. Instead, I had take notes while the teacher gave his lecture. Also, I had to learn to use a library. This was important because for most of my classes I needed to go to the library to do research. The second adjustment was to live on my own money. I had to manage my scholarship for my expenses. Before college, I never lived far from my parents, and I did not have to pay rent. Thus, at first I had trouble budgeting my money. For example, some money had to be kept for transportation, and I had to pay for meals and rent. In addition to that, I had to buy clothing, and sometimes I needed money for entertainment. Now, I still study in college, but fortunately the adjustments are over.

Hamidou Berthé
Mali

Worrying is a waste of time, and over a lifetime, worry will cost you years.

translated by
Pamela Liu
Taiwan (R.O.C.)

INFINITIVE VERBS

TO + (root form of the verb)			
(S)	*(V)*	*INFINITIVE*	*Complement*
I	learn**ed**	*TO SPEAK*	English.
He	expect**s**	*TO PASS*	the TOEFL exam.
She	like**s**	*TO READ*	poetry.
It	was a good day	*TO HAVE*	a picnic.
You	promis**ed**	*TO COME*	to her wedding.
We	agree**d**	*TO PLAY*	the piano.
They	continue	*TO TALK*	on the telephone.

Negative Verbs and the Infinitive

I	*did not* learn*	TO SPEAK	English.
He	*does not* expect*	TO PASS	the TOEFL exam.
She	*does not* like*	TO READ	poetry.
It	was *not* a good day	TO HAVE	a picnic.
You	*did not* promise*	TO COME	to her wedding.
We	*did not* agree*	TO PLAY	the piano
They	*do not* continue*	TO TALK	on the telephone.

*The root form of the verb is used with the negative.

Eating in the U.S.A.

One of the most distressing parts of culture shock I experienced in the United States was eating. Starting from the very beginning, when I was on the airplane, I remember that everything I ate was sour. I [did not want] TO TOUCH any of the food the next time it was served. After I landed, I went to a restaurant for my dinner. The waitress gave me a menu, but I could not order properly because I [did not know] which food was which. The only dish that I knew was beef steak, so I ordered a steak. I thought that I was finished ordering, but the waitress surprised me by asking a series of questions. "Do you want it rare, medium, or well done?" After that, she asked me about different kinds of salad dressing, dessert, and drink. At that time, I was very confused. Even now, I still [do not know] what "thousand island dressing" is. I still cannot order a meal comfortably because I have TO MAKE so many decisions. In Taiwan, if I go to a restaurant, I only need TO TELL the waitress the name of the dish because each dish has fixed ingredients. I [do not need] TO ANSWER questions, and I [do not need] TO MAKE thousands of decisions. TO SOLVE this problem in the United States, I have learned TO COOK my own meals.

Tai-Whang Chow
Taiwan

Read the paragraphs on the following page. Then do the exercises that follow.

I

The Problem of Language

The main problem I had when I _____ in the United States was the language. Of course, I knew this would happen, and I expected it. I _____ to the United States to study English, so I expected to have some language problems. However, I had been speaking English for a year, so I _____ the problems would be small. That was not true. I was not used to the accent people speak in this region, so I _____ a hard time understanding them. Also, the people _____ very quickly, and they did not pronounce some of the letters in the words. My friends _____ me that I would be able to understand the language better in a very short time—two or three weeks. Fortunately, they were correct. Now, after just one month, I understand much more, and I think, as my friends said, "It's just a matter of time."

VERBS: arrive come have speak tell think

Marcus Henrique Tessler
Brazil

___ EXERCISE 7A _____

1. Write the correct past tense verbs in the blanks. Use each verb on the list only once.
2. Circle 3 infinitive verbs in the paragraph.
3. What did Marcus find frustrating about the U.S.?
4. Have you ever felt the same way?

II

University Procedures

I needed to understand the procedures of the university. * I was confused about information about "credits" and required classes. I did not understand the registration process. In addition, the university system in American universities is very free. * Choosing a correct program of study is difficult. Another problem was that the Admissions Office did not know the education system in my country, Belgium, so I had to explain my complete background. Fortunately, I found two good ways to solve my problems. First, the Foreign Student Office was very helpful. Two people there spoke my language, French. * They listened to my problems and answered my questions. They also talked to the Admissions Office, and then they directed me to my "academic advisor." My advisor helped me to choose an appropriate program of study. * She advised me about the registration procedure. Therefore, I was able to enroll easily for this semester's classes.

Veronica Lenders
Belgium

___ EXERCISE 7B ___

1. Underline 5 infinitive verbs.

2. Circle at least 2 adjectives and 2 adverbs.

3. Join two clauses with ⌊, and⌋ , ⌊, but⌋ , or ⌊, so⌋ where you see the asterisks.

4. How did Veronica solve her problem?

III

Adjustment to Classes

I am adjusting to the new, exciting and frightening method of study in the United States. In addition to the language, there are many differences in the ways of teaching and learning between my country and the United States. For example, in the United States, some classes are lectures, some are discussion, and some are presentations. The instructors often encourage the students to express their ideas, and the students do not hesitate to do that. Also, the students are eager to get more knowledge, and the library is an important tool in successful learning. In my country, on the other hand, most classes are lectures. The instructors tell the students all the information. The students listen carefully to the lecture, and they write down what the instructor says. Some instructors allow students to express their ideas, but most students are reluctant to do this because they are afraid of making a mistake. Finally, in Thailand students do not usually use the library. Now that I am studying in the United States, I have to learn to adjust to the new experiences. I am learning to use the library, and sometimes I raise my hand and express myself in class. When I began my classes, the adjustment was very difficult, but now it is easier.

Pang Suwanchinda
Thailand

1. Circle 8 infinitive verbs.

2. Underline 3 present continuous verbs.

3. What is Pang learning to do?

4. Have you had a similar experience?

> In the sea of knowledge, diligence is the shore.
>
> translated by
> *Alice Lo*
> Hong Kong

—— **WRITING ASSIGNMENT** ——————————————————

Describe a problem that you had and an adjustment that you made when you entered a new situation. Use some of the questions below to help plan your paragraph.

What was the new situation?

Why were you involved in that situation?

What was puzzling? Strange? Unpleasant?

What was the problem?

Give an example of the problem.

How did you feel about the problem?

What adjustments did you make?

How did you solve the problem?

Did someone help you with the problem? How? In what ways?

Was your solution successful? How do you know?

What was the conclusion of the problem?

Exchange paragraphs with a classmate. Read the paragraph.

A. Circle the infinitive verbs.

B. Put parentheses around the adjectives.

C. What questions could you ask your classmate about the paragraph?

D. Underline any verb tense or spelling errors you see in the paragraph. Discuss these errors with your classmate.

HAVE TO, NEED TO, WANT TO

(S)	(V)	INFINITIVE	Complement
I	[have	TO] GO	to the supermarket.
I	[had	TO] GO	to the supermarket.
He	[needs	TO] STUDY	for the test.
She	[needed	TO] STUDY	for the test.
We	[want	TO] DRIVE	the new car.
They	[wanted	TO] DRIVE	the new car.

Negative Special Infinitive Verbs*

I	do not	[have	TO] GO	to the supermarket.
He	did not	[need	TO] STUDY	for the test.
We	do want	[want	TO] DRIVE	the new car.
They	did not	[used	TO] COOK	pizza.

*NOTE: The root form of the verb is used with the negative.

Special Infinitive Verb: USED TO (always in the past tense)

(S)	(V)	INFINITIVE	Complement
She	[used	TO] EAT	with her friends.
It	[used	TO] BE	easy to run fast.
You	[used	TO] WORK	at the Student Center.
They	[used	TO] COOK	pizza.

Interviews with Students

Students at a U.S. university were asked, "What did you used to do before you came to the U.S. that you don't do now?" Below are some of their replies.

"I didn't USED TO wear jeans in my country. I USED TO buy many clothes in Taipei. Here at the university, almost everyone wears blue jeans, so now I wear jeans, too."

Hui-Ching Chang
Taiwan (R.O.C.)

"I USED TO go to the movies, but now I don't because the movies are in English, so I can't understand them."

Abdirizak Osman
Somalia

"I USED TO eat goat's meat, but now I HAVE TO eat beef because goat's meat is difficult to buy."

Salem Gaddah
Morocco

"I USED TO go to the office every day, and I USED TO have a salary every month. Now I am a student, so I NEED TO pay bills."

Kuo Mei Ping Yu
Taiwan (R.O.C.)

"In my country, I USED TO drive a car, but now I don't. I didn't USED TO ride a bicycle, but now I do. I WANT TO drive a car, but I can't."

Mohamed Al-Souhibani
Saudi Arabia

"I USED TO visit my family every weekend, and I USED TO drink coffee at six o'clock with my mother. Now my family is far away, so I HAVE TO drink coffee with my friends."

Mohamed Gaddah
Morocco

"I USED TO have many friends in my country. I don't know many people here. I WANT TO meet people, but it is difficult."

Fawzia Hajc Essr
Somalia

"I USED TO smoke a lot, but cigarettes are very expensive here. It's also bad for my health."

Takeshi Kanome
Japan

> Don't kick against bricks.
>
> translated by
> *Fugimoto Akira*
> Japan

Read the paragraphs below. Then do the exercises that follow.

I

The Terrible Weather!

I am having trouble adjusting to the weather in Chicago. It is very cold. My friend, Carlos, _____ me that this winter has been one of the coldest since he _____ in Chicago. When I _____ to the university yesterday, my fingers and ears were freezing. I needed to buy winter clothing, so Carlos took me shopping after my class. I had to buy a hat, gloves, scarf, and moon boots. People call them moon boots because the astronauts wear them. Yesterday the temperature _____ minus eighteen degrees C, and today the temperature is minus seventeen degrees C. I also _____ to be careful of the snow and the ice wherever I walk. The weather here makes me walk fast because I want to go inside the heated buildings! I do not think I will adjust to this cold weather. Instead, I will wait for spring!

VERBS: arrive   be   have   tell   go

Maria Muñoz
Colombia

___ EXERCISE 7D _____

1. Write the correct past tense verbs in the blanks. Use each verb on the list only once.
2. Circle 3 special infinitive verbs: *have to, want to, need to.*

3. What is the main idea in this paragraph?

4. There is one sentence that could be taken out of this paragraph because it is not about the main idea. Which sentence is that? How do you know?

II

First Shopping Trip

My first shopping trip in the U.S. _____ a long time
take

and troubled me very much. It was the second morning after I arrived

in the United States. After breakfast, I _____ to the super-
go

market. When I _____ there, I _____ it was too early.
get   find

The market was not open, so I had to wait for one hour. When I

_____ the market, I did not know what to do with my bag.
enter

I wanted to ask, but I _____ ashamed. I decided to observe for
feel

a while, and I _____ around the store, trying to find everything
walk

that I wanted. Finally, I _____ a salesman for assistance, and
ask

he _____ me that I needed to look at the signs hanging above.
tell

I was very glad to find a lot of things that I was looking for. But another

trouble was the English names of the goods. Many names _____
be

very strange for me, so I _____ many things according to
buy

the pictures on the packages. I still made many mistakes. After I got

home, I found many things were not what I wanted. I think the first

time shopping was good practice for me. I _____ a lot, and
learn

now I am able to shop with confidence.

Shaoke Wang
China (P.R.C.)

1. Write the correct past tense verbs in the blanks.
2. Circle the special infinitive verbs: *have to, need to, want to.*
3. What problems did Wang have? How did he solve his problem?
4. Have you had a similar experience?

Reading thousands of books is good, but travelling thousands of miles is better.

translated by
Hsiang-Rwei Tseng
Taiwan (R.O.C.)

INTERVIEW

Ask a friend NOT in your class to describe several problems and solutions he or she had in a new situation. Discuss the problems, and choose one problem. Ask your friend to describe that problem more completely. Use some of the questions on page 166 to complete the interview. Use the chart below to help plan your paragraph.

PROBLEMS AND SOLUTIONS

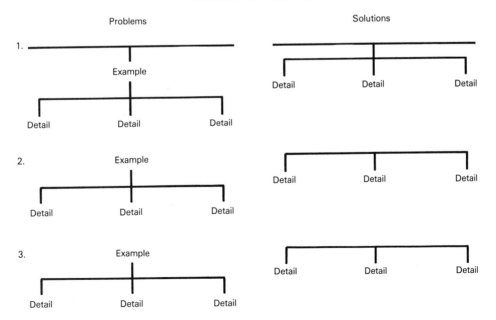

Write the paragraph. Use past tense verbs and correct subject and object pronouns. Use connectors and adjectives. In some sentences, use [, and] *,* [, but] *, or* [, so] *to join two clauses.*

Exchange paragraphs with a classmate. Read the paragraph.

A. What questions can you ask your classmate about the paragraph?

B. Underline any error you see in the paragraph: verb tense, pronoun, or spelling.

C. Discuss the errors with your classmate, and help your classmate correct the errors.

JOINING CLAUSES WITH BECAUSE

Subject + Verb (+ Complement)

BECAUSE

Subject + Verb (+Complement).

I was shocked <u>BECAUSE</u> people in the United States judge each

other strangely. U.S. professors grade students on class participation,

class discussion, and class presentations, so I am judged

incompetent <u>BECAUSE</u> I believe that "silence is golden." It

is painful for me to speak in class <u>BECAUSE</u> I grew up with Oriental

sayings such as, "The one who talks most must be the least learned,"

and "A big mouth is a big disaster." However, now I force

myself to speak <u>BECAUSE</u> class participation helps my grade.

Gwin Li
China (P.R.C.)

Read the personal letters on page 173. Then do the exercises that follow.

September 3, 198_

Dear Brother,

How are you? I am happy because my health is good, but I am sad because I am homesick. I hope all my brothers and sisters still remember me.

My English classes begin next week. However, I don't have enough money because I have to pay my rent. I need to have money to buy books, paper, and pens. I also want to buy the necessary study materials. Please tell our father about that.

I do not feel like a foreigner because the people are very nice. I am happy because I received a letter from you. Please write again.

Your brother,

Ameen Alawi
(United Arab Emirates)

___ EXERCISE 7F _____

1. Circle BECAUSE that joins two clauses.
2. Put parentheses around the special infinitives: *have to, need to, want to.*
3. Make the underlined sentences negative.
4. What are the reasons that Ameen is happy?

II

November 14, 198_

Dear Mother,

How are you? I am fine. ✳ I miss you. My dormitory is named Allison Hall. ✳ My roommate is a pretty girl whose name is Jill. The university is very big. ✳ I have to walk a lot. At first I was very tired because I had to walk so much, but now I like it.

There are people here from many parts of the world. I also have a Mexican friend. His name is Gerardo. ✳ He is from Texas. Please write me. Mom, could you send me some Mexican candy (pulpas, chilitos, and ticos)?

Thanks with love,

Pilar Ortiz
(Mexico)

1. Circle the <u>BECAUSE</u> that joins two clauses.
2. Join two clauses with $\boxed{, \text{and}}$, $\boxed{, \text{but}}$, or $\boxed{, \text{so}}$ where you see the asterisks.
3. What questions could Pilar's mother ask her?
4. What other information could Pilar include in her letter?

III

February 10, 198_

Dear Father,

I'm writing this letter for my writing course, so I am going to tell you about my English classes. I began my program last month. At that time, I took a language placement examination, and my teachers decided that I needed to take four courses because my language proficiency was low. These courses are: Writing, Grammar, Reading, and Oral Communication. My teachers in all of these classes are very intelligent and understanding, and the courses are useful and interesting. Oral Communication is difficult because in this course I have to talk to Americans, and sometimes I meet unsociable people.

Besides my four classes each day, I also have other scheduled classes. Here is copy of my weekly class schedule:

	M	T	W	R	F
8–8:50	Writing	Writing	Writing	Writing	Writing
9–9:50	Reading	Reading	Reading	Reading	Reading
10–10:50					
11–11:50	Grammar	Grammar	Grammar	Grammar	Grammar
12–1	LUNCH!	LUNCH!	LUNCH!	LUNCH!	LUNCH!
1–1:50	Language Laboratory	Language Laboratory	Language Laboratory	Language Laboratory	Language Laboratory
2–2:50	Oral Communication	Oral Communication	Oral Communication	Oral Communication	Oral Communication
3–3:50	Pronunciation		Pronunciation		Pronunciation
4–4:50		Typing	Culture	Typing	

As you can see, Father, I am very busy. I study all day, and I need to do at least two hours of homework each night. I used to have time for pleasures and for hobbies, but now I don't have any free time. However, I am learning many things about English because I want to succeed in my university work.

Your son,

Saud Al-Battal
(Saudi Arabia)

1. Circle <u>BECAUSE</u> that joins two clauses.

2. Underline 3 special infinitive verbs: *have to, need to,* and *used to.*

3. Why is Saud so busy?

4. Have you had a similar experience?

_____ **WRITING ASSIGNMENT** _____

Look at Saud's daily class schedule on page 174. Write a paragraph that describes Saud's schedule. Use present tense verbs and time connectors (first, next, then, after that, finally). Answer some of the questions below:

What time do Saud's classes begin?

What time does Saud have to get up? (probably)

What does Saud have to do every weekday (Monday through Friday)?

What classes does Saud have every day?

What other classes does Saud have?

When does he have those classes?

When does Saud arrive home from classes? (probably)

What does Saud do in the evening? (probably)

What time does Saud go to bed? (probably)

Rewrite the paragraph. Change the verbs to past tense.

> Many things look too difficult to complete,
> but if you persevere, you will be successful.
>
> translated by
> *Hui Ching Chiang*
> Taiwan (R.O.C.)

Read the paragraphs below. Then do the exercises that follow.

I

American Food

During the first month of my stay in the U.S., I had a very difficult time with American foods because I was not familiar with them, and their ingredients and cooking methods were different from those in Korea. Although I could have chosen to cook Korean foods myself, I wanted to stay in a commercial dormitory during the first semester, and I wanted to eat food in the dormitory cafeteria. Before I came to the U.S., I used to eat vegetable-based foods along with delicious Korean sauces. However, foods in the United States are mainly from animals, and sauces and dressings are different from those in Korea. For example, a typical meal in Korea consists of steamed sticky rice, a vegetable soup (Korean style), canned cabbage (*kimchi*), small dishes of fish or meat, and fresh vegetables with Korean sauces. A typical cafeteria meal in the United States consists of bread and potatoes, soup (American style), meat or fish, salads with dressings, and desserts. I had not eaten cereals for breakfast, or breads, or milk products (other than ice cream). What I could eat without hesitation were fried eggs, steak, and ice cream, although even the steaks did not taste good to me. Another embarrassing thing was that at first I did not know the names of most main dishes, and I could not imagine the taste of the foods. Therefore, I chose foods by pointing to them instead of calling them by name. Then I had to memorize the shape and/or color of foods and their taste, and to decide whether I could eat those again later or not. Fortunately, after the first month, the most difficult time passed, and I was able to choose foods I liked in the dormitory cafeteria.

Ray Cho
Korea

—— EXERCISE 71 ————————————————————

1. Underline 3 special infinitive verbs: *have to, used to, want to.*
2. Circle at least 6 adjectives in the paragraph.
3. Put parentheses around 5 connectors.
4. How did Ray solve his problem?

II

How Much? How Many?

"How many is it?"
"How many? As many as you want to buy!"
"But, no. I mean, which is the cost?"
"I don't know. I'm just selling them."

"I mean, how many dollars do I have to give you for it?"

"Oh! You mean, 'How MUCH is it?' O.K.! It is three dollars each."

"Oh—O.K."

For me, each conversation like this one, especially with someone from the U.S., represents a headache. I know grammar and vocabulary, and I put the words together as I learned in my English classes. But sometimes I forget a word, and . . . then I have troubles. Nobody understands me. I have to be thinking each moment about what I am saying. However, it is easier if I am talking to people who are also foreign in this country and are not English speakers. They are living my same experiences, so they understand the effort I am making with each phrase that I build up. If I make a mistake, they try to see what happened. Perhaps I am pronouncing a word in the wrong way, but communication can still go on. That is not the case when I am talking to U.S. citizens. They think they are wasting too much time in a conversation, or they think that I am stupid because I do not even know how to speak. I think this problem arises because U.S. citizens do not travel a lot outside their own country, so they are not in touch with other languages and cultures. I am sure that once a person goes to another country and has to talk in a foreign language, he or she will understand foreigners better. Then he or she will have the patience and the willingness to communicate with other people.

Maria Isabel DiMare
Costa Rica

____ EXERCISE 7J _____

1. Underline the present continuous verbs in the paragraph.

2. Circle the BECAUSE that joins two clauses.

3. Put parentheses around 5 prepositional phrases.

4. Have you had an experience similar to Maria's?

III

Competition

The process of adjusting to American culture during my first months in the United States was very distressing because I was raised in a society where the sharing of lives is vital. American people live their own lives. * They do not share spontaneously with other people. I had imagined them as more friendly people. * I found myself in the middle of a cold atmosphere. One example of the attitude in the United States

_____ the competition among university classmates. In graduate classes, the final grades people receive are usually based on the percentage of the rest of the group. This grading system _____ to complete isolationism among individuals because nobody can know, before an exam, what kind and what volume of information his classmates have. Having more information for an exam than the other people in the class makes one get a higher grade. Therefore, no one _____ his information or _____ with his classmates. These things made me feel unhappy until the day a classmate said "Hi!" and smiled at me. I realized then that the competition in the classroom does not need to interfere with friendship. ∗ I have been much happier.

VERBS: be   lead   share   study

Jorge Lopez Rendón
Colombia

___ EXERCISE 7K _____

1. Write the correct present tense verbs in the blanks. Use each verb on the list only once.
2. Join 2 clauses with |, and| or |, but| where you see the asterisks (∗).
3. Circle at least 2 adjectives and 2 adverbs.
4. What do you remember about Jorge's paragraph?

> The depth of the sea can be predicted,
> but the depth of the heart: who knows?
>
> translated by
> *Ju Lun Lo*
> Indonesia

Read the paragraph on the next page. Notice how clauses are joined with |, and|, |, but|, |, so|, *and* |because|.

Commercial Centers in the United States

The most surprising thing about Gainesville, Florida in comparison with my hometown in Belgium is the quantity of commercial centers. During my first week in the United States, I walked down College Avenue. I had an endless choice of business centers , <u>AND</u> each had a huge supermarket. I was not used to this luxury and abundance , <u>SO</u> I was very confused. In my hometown, we do not even have a shopping center. The small country village has only small shops , <u>SO</u> buying groceries is a big event. I have to go from the bakery to the butcher, and from the cheese shop to the vegetable shop. I talk with the shop owners , <u>AND</u> I buy what I need. The entire trip takes most of a morning <u>BECAUSE</u> I have to go to so many shops. In the United States, I go shopping , <u>BUT</u> it does not take longer than one hour. The supermarket has all the items I want to buy in one store. It even has drugs and hardware for sale. I must admit that for students or bachelors, the supermarket is very practical , <u>BUT</u> it is certainly not as enjoyable as the more personalized shopping in my hometown.

André Emsens
Belgium

___ EXERCISE 7L _____

Read the paragraphs below. Join some of the clauses together with |, and| *,* |, but| *,* |, so| *, or* |because| *. Join the clauses where you see the asterisks (*).*

I

How My Life Has Changed

My life has changed twice during the last three years. In my country, high school graduates have to serve in the National Guard for 26 months. I had no choice. * I followed my fortune. I entered the army at the age of twenty-two. The first change I had to face was that as a soldier, I had to obey orders with a smile. * I had to carry out the missions assigned by my superiors. Failure is not accepted in the army. * It is punished. I had to awake at 5:30 A.M. * That was my official schedule. I had to get washed, shaved, and dressed in my green uniform within fifteen minutes. After breakfast, from 6:00 A.M. until 7 P.M., I worked very hard at my job. * I trained with guns. Even my bedtime was regulated by my superiors. Today, on the contrary, no one tells me what to do! As a university student, I am completely responsible for my schedule. * I do not have to obey orders. Therefore, I never get up before 8 A.M. * I choose the time to have breakfast. Until lunch, I use my time to attend classes, to sport around, to go shopping, or to sleep. In the afternoon, I study, rest, or even work on a computer. At night, I can do anything I feel like: go to a movie, watch television, listen to music, or talk with my friends. I can finally wear the clothes I want: jeans, a three-piece suit, or shorts! In conclusion, even though I believe in the defense of my country, I prefer the life of a student!

Pavlos G. Alexandros
Cyprus

II

Cultural Change

Having consecutive classes during lunchtime was the most distressing change for me. I had visited the U.S. before. * The American way of life was familiar to me. However, when I _____ attending classes, I _____ that the continuous daily working schedule from 8 A.M. to 5 P.M. was something I _____ not accustomed to. In my university job in Venezuela, the work schedule is from 8 to 12 and from 2 to 6. Here in the United States, the regular lunchtime is from 12 to 1. * People in my country usually have lunch between 12 and 2. Unfortunately, my fall semester schedule _____ consecutive classes at noon and at 1 P.M. * That really distressed me terribly. I could not understand why people here needed to have class lectures at noon, much less two consecutive classes. Consequently, the students cannot have lunch at the regular time. In my culture, lunchtime is usually respected. In addition, I need to have meals at very regular times. * I have strict medical instructions. Therefore, I had a very difficult time adjusting to the new schedule.

VERBS: be   include   realize   start

Lucas Alvarez-Martinez
Venezuela

III

Relationships

In the past few months, my feelings about the relationship between my professors and me have changed a lot. In my country, I always thought that all of my professors were perfect. I felt that they never made any mistakes, even when my good friend told me that he knew that my professor had made some mistakes. I never asked questions when I did not understand the lecture. ∗ I was afraid that I would say something wrong. I only talked to my professors a few times. ∗ I was afraid I would make them dislike me. In contrast, I feel very different now. I really feel much more comfortable when I talk to my professors. ∗ I realize that sometimes I make mistakes, and sometimes my professors make mistakes, too. Now, when I talk to my professors, I feel like I am talking to my good friend. ∗ It is much easier to learn from a friend. The relationship between my professors and me has changed. ∗ I learn more from school than ever.

Mai Anh Tran
Vietnam

___ WRITING ASSIGNMENT _____

Write a paragraph about how your life changed because of a new situation or a new place. Use the chart below to plan your paragraph.

How My Life Has Changed

EFFECT:

    the change in my life _____

_____

CAUSE(S):

    why the change occurred _____

_____

    the change in my life was good because _____

_____

_____

the change in my life was not good because _____

_____

_____

RESULTS:

the result(s) of the change in my life _____

_____

_____

___ **WRITING ASSIGNMENT** _____

You have invited a classmate to your apartment (or house or dormitory) for dinner. Draw a map that shows your friend how to get from your classroom to your home. Then exchange maps with that classmate. Use your classmate's map to write a paragraph about how to get from your classroom to your classmate's home. Answer some of the questions below to plan your paragraph. Use time connectors and present tense verbs in the paragraph. If necessary, ask your classmate questions about his or her map to complete your paragraph.

How far is it to your classmate's home?

How will you get to his or her home? (By car? By bus? By walking?)

When you leave your classroom building, what should you do first? (Turn right? Walk one block north? Drive two miles east?)

What street should you go to?

Then what should you do?

After that? Then?

Finally?

Exchange paragraphs with your classmate:

A. Read the paragraph.

B. Is is a correct description of how to get to your home?

C. What changes are necessary in the paragraph to make it correct?

D. Underline any errors you find in the paragraph: verb tense, pronouns, or spelling.

E. Discuss the errors with your classmate, and correct the errors.

Study the chart below. It gives recent trends of computer sales in the United States, and it predicts future computer sales (see the asterisk). Write a paragraph that describes the chart. Use present and past tense verbs, prepositions, and connectors. Use some of the sentence structures below.

According to a survey by *Creative Computing* magazine, . . .

Before 1980, computer sales . . .

However, during the next few years, . . .

For example, computers sold to businesses . . .

In addition, computers sold for home use . . .

Schools also bought computers, but . . .

The survey predicts that . . . will be sold . . .

I think the reason(s) for the recent trends in U.S. computer sales is/are . . .

NUMBERS OF PERSONAL COMPUTERS IN THE U.S.A.

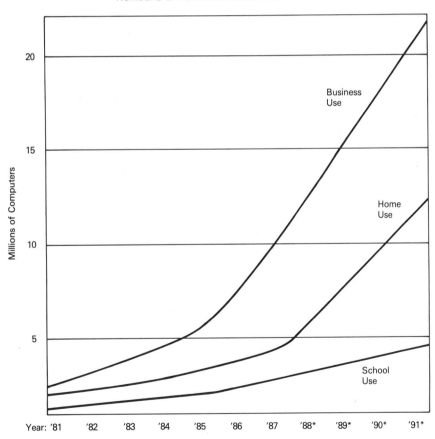

*Predicted

OTHER WRITING TOPICS

A Problem I Encountered Last Year

An Adjustment I Made in Childhood

A Dream I Had

My Favorite Activities in My Country

My Favorite Activities in the United States

A Person Who Changed My Life

WRITING PROJECTS

Individual Project

Write several paragraphs about changes that have happened to you because of a change in your life situation. Then submit the paragraphs to a student newspaper, or make a booklet entitled "Adjustments." Illustrate the booklet with "before" and "after" drawings, charts, and photographs.

Group Project

Construct a housing survey like the one below. Ask international students NOT in your class to complete copies of the survey. Compile the surveys, and summarize the data in several paragraphs. Submit the results of the survey to the university Housing Office or the Foreign Student Office for incoming international students to use.

SAMPLE QUESTIONNAIRE

Country _____

M _____   F _____

Single _____   Married _____   Children _____

Age _____   Graduate _____   Undergraduate _____

I LIVE IN

_____ an apartment _____ a house _____ a dorm room

I LIVE

_____ alone _____ with a roommate(s) _____ with my family

_____ with an American family _____ other

How would you recommend your living situation to another international student?

_____ Excellent _____ Good _____ Bad

Advantages of where you live:

	excellent	good	not too important
Low rent			
Food prepared			
Kept clean			
Close to campus			
Good roommate(s)			
Live alone			
Quiet			
Beautiful surroundings			

Disadvantages of where you live:

	terrible	bad	not too important
High rent			
Prepare my own food			
Clean it myself			
Far from campus			
Bad roommate(s)			
Live alone			
Noisy			
Ugly			

Eight

Similarities
and Differences

Breakfasts

Breakfast in my country is completely different from breakfast in the U.S. In Malaysia, for example, we eat the same foods for breakfast that we eat for lunch or for dinner: rice, meat, and vegetables. We do not specify what kind of food is suitable for breakfast. However, after I arrived in the U.S., I learned that Americans have very specific foods for breakfast: eggs, toast, pancakes, and juice. Another difference I discovered when I came to the United Sates was the attitude towards milk. In my country, if someone drinks milk in the morning, we say that he is poisoning his body. We think milk is very bad for our health. In the U.S., however, people drink milk every morning, and they believe that milk is "the most perfect food." I am very confused about these differences, but I am sure I will adjust to them.

Chia-Chon Pin
Malaysia

Light your own house before you light the others.

translated by
Jamal Jawad
Sierra Leone

TIME CLAUSES

Time Words: **BEFORE**   **AFTER**   **WHEN**

TIME WORD + S + V (+ C), S + V (+ C).

OR

S + V (+ C) TIME WORD + S + V (+ C).

Examples

[WHEN] I go to the supermarket, I buy many foods.

OR

I buy many foods [WHEN] I go to the supermarket.

[BEFORE] I came to the U.S., I never watched television.

OR

I never watched television [BEFORE] I came to the U.S.

[AFTER] I finish my university work, I will be an engineer.

OR

I will be an engineer [AFTER] I finish my university work.

Breakfast

BEFORE I left Japan, I did not think about American food. But WHEN I was on the jet, the flight attendant brought me a very strange breakfast. I had a cup of coffee, cookies, bread and butter, and some fruit. The meal was so simple that I was not completely satisfied. I wanted to have another meal soon. In Japan, we have rice, miso-soup, tofu (soybean pudding), and some pickles for breakfast. We often put some sea food into the miso-soup, such as octopus, seaplant, seafly, or seaworm. AFTER we finish breakfast in Japan, we feel satisfied because the meal is light, not greasy, and good for our health.

Misuaki Uchida
Japan

Time always puts things in the right place.

translated by
Fausto Ibarra
Mexico

Read the paragraphs below. Then do the exercises that follow.

I

Breakfast Differences

There _____ several differences between breakfast in my country and breakfast in the U.S. First, before I came to the United States, I ate breakfast with my family every day. Now, I _____ alone, so I often _____ television when I eat my breakfast. Second, in my country, Venezuela, people usually _____ at 6 A.M. because they begin work at 7 A.M. However, in the U.S., people _____ to work at 9 A.M., so they usually eat breakfast later. Finally, people in my country always _____ breakfast because they think that it is the most important meal of the day. However, in the

United States, people sometimes do not have breakfast. They drink coffee, but they do not eat anything.

VERBS: be   begin   eat   lie   watch

Raquel Pedroza
Venezuela

____ Exercise 8A _____

1. Write the correct present tense verbs in the blanks. Use each verb on the list only once.
2. Underline the time clauses in the paragraph. Circle the time word in each clause: WHEN, BEFORE, AFTER.
3. Put parentheses around 4 adverbs of frequency.
4. Do you think that Raquel prefers breakfast in Venezuela or breakfast in the U.S.? Why?

II

Breakfast in My Country and in the United States

In my country, breakfast is not the same as it is in the United States. When I _____ in my country, I _____ a small breakfast of hot milk, coffee, fresh bread, jelly, butter, and cheese. Every day I _____ almost the same foods. However, after I _____ in the United States, I _____ that breakfast is a much more important meal. I live with an American family, and every morning we have a large meal. We eat bacon and eggs, toast, butter and jelly, cottage cheese, coffee or tea, cold milk, and orange juice. Before I _____ to the United States, I never _____ that breakfast was a very interesting or important meal, but now I have changed my mind, and I enjoy eating breakfast.

VERBS: arrive   be   come   eat   find   have   think

Marléne Clerc
Switzerland

1. Write the correct past tense verbs in the blanks. Use each verb on the list only once.
2. Underline 3 time clauses in the paragraph. Circle the time word in each clause: WHEN, BEFORE, AFTER.
3. Put parentheses around at least 5 adjectives.
4. What are the differences between breakfast in Switzerland and breakfast in the United States?

> The frugal man eats his dinner twice.
>
> translated by
> *Youssef El-Tayash*
> Libya

COMPARATIVE ADJECTIVES*

S + V + short ADJECTIVE + -ER + (THAN + C)

Lorena is	TALLER	THAN Faiza.
The small class was	QUIETER	THAN the large class.
This test seemed	EASIER	THAN that one.
He ran	FASTER	THAN his brother,
and he is	STRONGER, too.	

S + V + MORE (LESS) + long ADJECTIVE + (THAN + C)

Maria's book is MORE INTERESTING THAN mine.

Learning English is MORE DIFFICULT THAN learning Spanish.

Supermarkets in the United States are MORE CONVENIENT THAN grocery stores in my country, but they are also MORE EXPENSIVE.

NOTE: See the spelling rules in Appendix C.

Two Food Stores

One difference between Boston and my hometown, Yaizu, is the size of the food stores. For example, Safeway, which is one of the grocery stores in Boston, has a huge parking lot in front of the building because many customers drive their cars to the store. A lot of carts are at the entrance of the supermarket, so it is easy for people to buy many groceries just once a month. Inside the supermarkets, the aisles occupy a large part of the room, so people can shop comfortably. In contrast, Yakumo Store, one of the grocery stores in Yaizu, is much <u>SMALLER THAN</u> Safeway, and it is also <u>LESS COMFORTABLE</u>. Yakumo Store does not have a parking lot because most customers come from neighboring houses. Also, customers use small, hand-carried baskets because they usually buy food for only one or two days. The size of the store is a quarter of Safeway. A lot of food is crammed into the refrigerators and the shelves, so the store is <u>LESS CONVENIENT THAN</u> Safeway. However, the customers take only ten or twenty minutes to buy food for that evening, so the convenience is not important. Finally, both Safeway and Yakumo Store serve their customers adequately, but I think Safeway has <u>MORE PLEASANT</u> surroundings.

Hidekazu Oishi
Japan

Read the paragraphs below. Then do the exercises that follow.

I

Shopping in the U.S. and Paraguay

There are several differences between shopping for food in my country and shopping for food in the U.S. First, in Paraguay, there are many small stores around the city, so I do not have to travel to buy food. In the U.S., however, the supermarkets are fewer and larger, and they are not located in neighborhoods where people live. Therefore, I must drive my car to the supermarket. Second, the time for shopping in Paraguay and in the U.S. differs. In my country, people usually go to the food stores after they have finished their jobs, in the first hours of the night. In contrast, people in the U.S. are accustomed to shopping when they have more time. They usually go to the supermarkets on the weekends, especially on Saturday morning, and they even shop on Sundays. Finally, people in Paraguay and the U.S. shop for different amounts of food. In my country, the selection of foods is smaller, and the foods are much fresher than foods in the U.S. supermarkets. Moreover, many people in Paraguay are not able to preserve their food because they do not have refrigerators, so they buy only enough food for the day. In contrast, people in the United States often buy canned and frozen foods that they can keep for several weeks or months, so their shopping trips are more efficient and more complete.

César Prieto
Paraguay

—— EXERCISE 8C ————————————————

1. Underline 4 short comparative adjectives and 2 long comparative adjectives in the paragraph.
2. Put 2 time clauses in parentheses, and circle the time word in each clause.
3. What does César prefer about shopping in Paraguay?
4. What does he prefer about shopping in the United States?

II

Differences in Shopping

My country, Sudan, is poorer than the U.S. * There are differences between shopping for food there and shopping for food in the U.S. When I came to the U.S., the supermarkets surprised me because they sell everything. In my country, I have to go to many stores to collect the foods I need because the stores belong to individual persons, and they do not have much money to buy many foods. But the U. S. supermarket is much more convenient. I can buy meat, bread, vegetables, drugs, auto supplies, and even clothing at just one large store. I was also surprised at the hours for shopping in the U.S. The supermarkets are almost always open. * In my country, I have to shop during specific hours because the food comes from the rural areas. There are no refrigerators for storage. * The food is limited. For example, if I want to buy fresh vegetables, I need to go to the store early. Finally the supermarkets in the U.S. have a much larger selection of foods. * I can always find what I want to buy. In my country, I have fewer choices. For all these reasons, I think that U.S. supermarkets are richer and more developed than food stores in Sudan.

Tarig Ahmed Habbas
Sudan

—— EXERCISE 8D ————————————————

1. Underline 4 short comparative adjectives and 2 long comparative adjectives in the paragraph.

2. Join 2 clauses with $\boxed{\text{, but}}$, $\boxed{\text{, so}}$, or $\boxed{\text{because}}$ wherever you see an asterisk (*).

3. Put parentheses around the special verbs: *have to, want to, need to.*

4. In what ways is Tarig's paragraph similar to César's and Hidekazu's paragraphs (above)? In what ways is it different?

The faster you run, the faster you die.

translated by
Claude Kambou
Burkina Faso

__ WRITING ASSIGNMENT _____

*Choose two stores, or two **kinds** of stores, that you have in your country. Write a paragraph that describes the similarities and the differences between the 2 stores. Use short and long comparative adjectives, and use some time clauses.*

Examples

2 food stores	OR	1 department store *and* 1 gift shop
2 clothing stores	OR	1 fruit store *and* 1 bakery
2 open-air markets	OR	???????????????

In your paragraph, use some of the following structures:

COMPARISON STRUCTURES

X is	AS tall	AS	Y.
X is	SIMILAR TO		Y.
X is	THE SAME AS		Y.
BOTH X	and Y are . . .		
LIKE X,	Y is . . .		
There are	SIMILARITIES BETWEEN	X and Y.	

X is DIFFERENT FROM Y.

X is DIFFERENT THAN Y.

X DIFFERS FROM Y.

There are several DIFFERENCES BETWEEN X and Y.

Use the chart below to plan your paragraph.

Two Stores

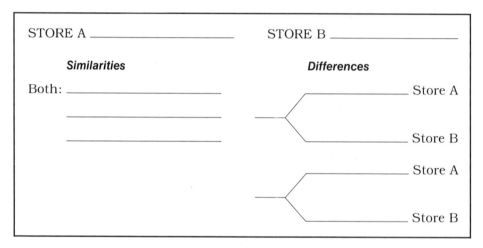

STORE A _____   STORE B _____

Similarities   *Differences*

Both: _____   _____ Store A

_____

_____   _____ Store B

_____ Store A

_____ Store B

Exchange paragraphs with a classmate. Read the paragraph.

    A. Circle the short and long comparative adjectives.

    B. Put parentheses around the time clauses.

    C. Put brackets [ ] around the connectors in the paragraph.

    D. Underline any errors you see in the paragraph. Discuss these errors with your classmate, and help correct the errors.

___ **INTERVIEW**  _____

Ask a person NOT in your class and NOT from your country to describe a food store in his or her country. Make a chart like the one above, and write the similarities and differences between that person's description and a food store in your country. Then write a paragraph that compares the two stores. Use comparative adjectives and some of the structures above.

S + V + **THE** + short **ADJECTIVE** + **-EST** (+ C).

Medhi	is	THE TALLEST	man in the class.
Morella	is	THE HAPPIEST	
	and	THE PRETTIEST	girl in her family.
The trip	was	THE LONGEST	we had taken.
They	carried	THE HEAVIEST	box upstairs.

S + V + **THE** + MOST (LEAST) + long **ADJECTIVE** (+ C).

We were THE MOST WORRIED passengers on the airplane.

Finding an apartment was THE MOST FRUSTRATING job I ever had.

Hassan is THE MOST SUCCESSFUL graduate student of all.

Her flower garden is THE BRIGHTEST
and THE MOST FRAGRANT.

EXCEPTIONS

	Comparison between 2	Comparison among 3 or more
GOOD:	BETTER THAN	THE BEST
BAD:	WORSE THAN	THE WORST

Examples

Man-Chiu played soccer BETTER THAN Elmi.

Professor Berry was THE BEST teacher I have had.

The statistics exam was WORSE THAN the math exam.

That was THE WORST experience I ever faced.

Teachers

I have attended schools in three countries—Colombia, Mexico, and the United States—and my opinion is that North American teachers are THE MOST FRIENDLY, Mexican teachers are THE STRICTEST, and Colombian teachers are THE LEAST SENSITIVE. In their attitudes towards their jobs, teachers in these countries are very different. In Colombia, most of the teachers are people whose main purpose is far from teaching. These teachers look at their jobs as something worthless, and they look at their students as another piece of furniture in the classroom. In Mexico, the teachers are very strict. For example, even if you pass your exams, if your behavior is not good, you will not pass to the next level. The situation is different in the U.S. North American teachers look at their students as intelligent beings, and they worry about their students. There is not much distance between the teachers and their students, and some teachers let their students call them by their first names!

Graciano Calderon
Colombia

To meet someone by chance is sometimes better than a thousand appointments.

translated by
Joharah Nihidh
Saudi Arabia

Read the paragraphs below. Then do the exercises that follow.

I

Teachers

In my country, teachers are the most important workers for the community. They have the highest salaries and the shortest time of working. However, I have learned that teachers in the United States do not have as much income as teachers in Kuwait. * They work harder and longer hours. Another difference is that in Kuwait, we do not have any women teachers in men's schools. * In the United States, many teachers are women. I find this very strange and unusual. Finally, in my country, teachers have a stronger relationship with their students than teachers in the United States. I think that this is because of the shared language and because of the longer time that students study with their teachers. In Kuwait, teachers teach their students all day for a year. * In the United States, students meet with several teachers, one for each class. * Classes last a shorter time, sometimes only two months. For these reasons, I prefer the teachers in Kuwait.

Naser Al-Gabandi
Kuwait

_____ EXERCISE 8E _____

1. Underline 5 comparative adjectives in the paragraph.

2. Put parentheses around the negative verbs.

3. Put brackets around 5 prepositional phrases. Circle the noun (or the pronoun) that follows each preposition.

4. Join 2 sentences with $\boxed{\text{, and}}$ or $\boxed{\text{, but}}$ where you see the asterisks [*].

II

Differences Between Teachers

I think that there are many differences between teachers in the United States and teachers in my country. <u>First, U.S. teachers are more involved in their teaching than the teachers in Iraq.</u> I think this is because teachers in my country must teach more than thirty students in a class, but in my U.S. classes there are only ten to twelve students. <u>Second, U.S. teachers are freer in their methods than Iraqi teachers.</u> Iraqi teachers have fixed schedules and classical methods, but U.S. teachers use techniques like role-playing and equipment like computers. <u>Finally, the most important difference between U.S. teachers and Iraqi teachers is their evaluation procedures.</u> In my country, students must pass only one examination, but in the United States, students have many assignments and quizzes, so their success depends on many different things.

Hatim Al-Kinani
Iraq

_____ EXERCISE 8F _____

1. Put parentheses around 3 comparative adjectives.

2. Circle 3 connectors in the paragraph.

3. Identify the subject and the verb in the underlined sentences.

4. Compare and contrast Hatim's paragraph with Naser's paragraph (Paragraph II). In what ways are their ideas similar? In what ways are they different?

> It is better to study nothing than to study a lot without thinking.
>
> translated by
> *John Shyh-Yuan Wang*
> China (P.R.C.)

Write a paragraph about the best teacher *OR* the best class *you have had. Answer some of the questions below to plan your paragraph. Use comparative adjectives, and give examples to show why you chose that teacher (or class).*

Who was your best teacher? OR

Which class was your best class?

What qualities made that teacher (or class) the best?

Why did you especially like that teacher (or class)?

because _____

For example, _____

_____

because _____

For example, _____

_____

because _____

For example, _____

_____

The monk from far away knows much more about the Bible than the monk who lives here.

translated by
Hsiang-Rwei Tseng
Taiwan (R.O.C.)

___ WRITING ASSIGNMENT _____

Study the chart on page 199. Answer the questions that follow. Then write a paragraph about prices for food in Atlanta and prices for food in your hometown. Use comparative adjectives.

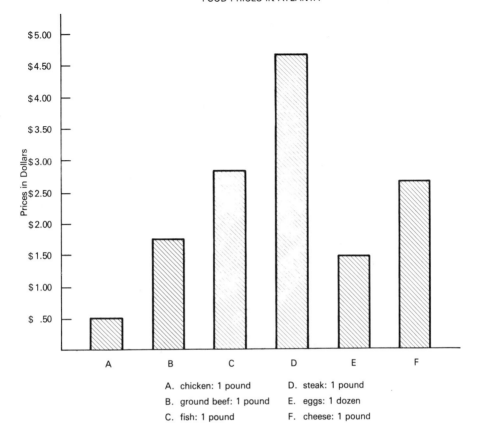

FOOD PRICES IN ATLANTA

A. chicken: 1 pound   D. steak: 1 pound
B. ground beef: 1 pound   E. eggs: 1 dozen
C. fish: 1 pound   F. cheese: 1 pound

QUESTIONS

1. What foods are cheaper than fish?
2. What is the most expensive food on the chart?
3. What is the cheapest food on the chart?
4. What foods are more expensive than cheese?
5. Are the foods in Atlanta more expensive than the same foods in your hometown?
6. What foods in Atlanta are too expensive to buy?
7. What foods are good bargains?
8. Do you buy chicken? Beef? Eggs? Why? Why not?
9. Where do you shop for food in your hometown?
10. What does the store look like?
11. Where is it located?
12. What foods are available in the store?

Read the paragraphs below. Join two clauses with [, and] , [, but] , [, so] , or [because] wherever you see an asterisk.

I

Television

There are two great differences between television in my country, which is Tunisia, and television in the U.S. For example, in Tunisia, we have fewer channels (only 2). The first is in Arabic * The second is in French. In the U.S., however, there are so many channels that I cannot count them. * All of them are in English. Of course, in Tunisia, we can watch a lot of channels from Italy. * The programs are in Italian. * When we watch, we do not understand anything. Before I came to the U.S., I used to watch soccer matches in Italian because I did not need to listen to the language. I also watched some films in Italian. * I had already seen them in French. The other most essential difference between television in Tunisia and television in the U.S. is the ownership of the television stations. Tunisian television is controlled by the government. * There are many political programs that deal with the party that is governing the country. In contrast, U.S. television is privately owned. The stations broadcast many, many advertisements to earn money. * They are less interested in politics. I do not like the interruptions of these advertisements. * I prefer television in my country.

Sofouen Ben Brahim
Tunisia

II

Similarities in Television Programs

In Mexico City, many television programs are the same as those in the U.S., but there are some differences. For example, many of the television series are the same. * They are spoken in Spanish instead of English. We have dramas and news, sports and movies on Mexican television. Of course, some programs are different. For example, on game shows in both countries, the purpose is for the contestants to win money. * On the U.S. game shows, you need more luck, while on Mexican game shows, you need more agility. Finally, Mexico City has cablevision just like the U.S. * We have many channels. Some are in English. * Many children learn English by watching TV. Some of the channels have special programs just for children. * On other channels, there are just movies or just sports. In short, television in my country is similar to television in the U.S.

Elias Rodriquez
Mexico

Read the paragraphs below about various aspects of U.S. life that students found different from their home countries. Then do the exercises that follow.

I

Transportation

Although my hometown Ipoh, and Pocatello, both have bus transportation, the use of mass transportation in the two cities is very different. Middle-income residents in Ipoh use the buses more often than people in Pocatello because the buses in Ipoh are more numerous and operate more efficiently. For example, buses in Ipoh do not stop at every busy stop. They stop when there are customers who want to board the buses. Furthermore, residents in Ipoh only have to wait ten minutes at the most before the bus arrives, so they will usually get to work on time. In addition, the price of the bus fare is only twenty cents (in American currency). On the other hand, buses in Pocatello stop at every bus stop, even when no one wants to leave or board the bus. Moreover, residents have to wait at least thirty minutes before they can catch the next bus. As a result, many people arrive late to their appointments and are more frustrated than people in Ipoh. Finally, the bus fare in Pocatello is much more expensive: fifty cents. For these reasons, I prefer the buses in Ipoh to the buses in Pocatello.

Chee Siou
Malaysia

___ EXERCISE 8H ___

1. Put brackets around the comparison and contrast structures in the first sentence of the paragraph.

2. Underline 4 time clauses. Identify the subject (S) and the verb (V) in each time clause.

3. Put parentheses around 5 comparative adjectives in the paragraph.

4. Circle 6 connectors in the paragraph. Identify each connector as a connector of additional information OR contrasting information OR cause-effect information.

II

Americans and Their Pets

After I had lived in Taiwan for twenty years, I was quite surprised to see that the American people are much more affectionate toward their pets than people in my country. Two years ago, when I first arrived in the United States, I took a walk to the small park near my house. I saw several people playing games with their pets, and if their pets did a good job, their masters would reward them with food or even with kisses. There were also people carefully combing their dogs' hair or clipping their dogs' nails. I had never seen that in my life! Therefore, I was totally dumbfounded. Later, when I was at the supermarket, I saw a multitude of frivolous and crazy pet foods and cosmetics: dog shampoo, kitty candy, pet clippers, and jeweled cat collars. I was shocked by how much care people showed toward their pets. Compared to the treatment pets get in my country, animals in America live a life of luxury. In Taiwan, people are much less concerned about their pets. For example, we do not produce any special pet food for pets. People usually feed pets with their leftovers, and they do not give their pets special treats. In fact, people in Taiwan do not allow their pets to enter their houses. No matter how bad the weather is, the pets always have to stay outside. Finally, people in my country would *never kiss* their animals!

Hsiu-Yueh Chiu
Taiwan (R.O.C.)

—— EXERCISE 8I ——————————————————————

1. Underline 2 comparative adjectives in the paragraph.
2. Circle 3 adjectives and 3 adverbs.
3. Put parentheses around 3 time clauses.
4. Put brackets around 4 adverbs of frequency.

III

Traffic Rules

When I first came to Ashland, I noticed how different the traffic in the downtown area was from my home city, Bangladore. Even though there are many traffic rules in Bangladore, not one person follows them. But here, in

Ohio, most people follow the traffic regulations. For example, they stop at every stop sign, even in the middle of the night when there is no traffic at all. Back home, the streets are much narrower compared to the broad roads in Ashland. Moreover, in downtown Bangladore, lots of people walk in the streets instead of the footpaths (sidewalks) because the footpaths are often used as parking spaces for scooters and motorcycles (and at times, cars as well!). However, in downtown Ashland, the sidewalks are used for people to walk, and parking spaces for vehicles are provided in the center of the streets. Another difference between these two cities is that there are no buses allowed in the downtown area of Bangladore, but quite a few buses go through the wide streets in Ashland. Finally, the overall scene in Bangladore is one of noise and crowds: lots of bullock carts transporting goods, car horns honking all the time, and many, many people. But here in Ashland, it is very quiet and peaceful in the downtown area, and horns are used only to greet friends.

Kamala Vedanthan
Bangladesh

_____ EXERCISE 8J _____

1. Circle the pronouns in the paragraph. Identify the subject pronouns (S), and the object pronouns (O).

2. Underline at least 5 prepositional phrases in the paragraph.

3. Put parentheses around at least 5 connectors in the paragraph. Identify each connector as an additional information OR a contrasting OR a cause-effect connector.

4. Put brackets around 1 comparative adjective in the paragraph.

> A tick far across the ocean can clearly be seen, but an elephant in front of the eyes can't be seen.
>
> translated by
> *Ju Lun Lo*
> Indonesia

_____ INTERVIEW   _____

Ask a person NOT in your class to describe several similarities and differences between his or her country and another country. Discuss what similarity or difference would be most interesting to write about. Ask some of the questions on page 204, and use the chart on page 204 to help plan your paragraph.

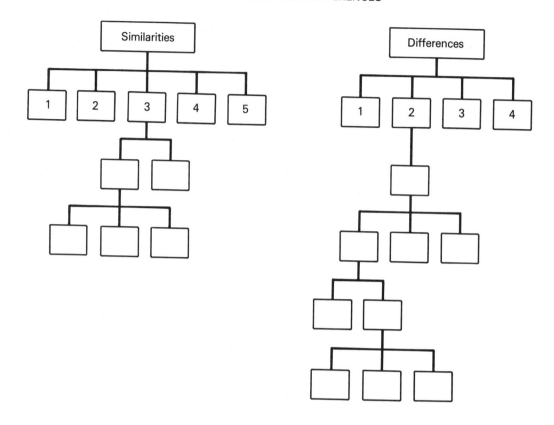

What are some similarities you noticed?

What are some differences?

What ONE similarity or difference was the most memorable?

What made it memorable? Give an example.

Why do you remember it? Give another example.

Write the paragraph. Use comparison and/or contrast structures. Use past tense, and use connectors.

Exchange paragraphs with a classmate. Read the paragraph.

    A. Put parentheses around any comparison or contrast structures.

    B. Circle the connectors in the paragraph.

    C. Underline errors you find in the paragraph.

    D. Discuss those errors with your classmate, and help correct the errors.

Read the paragraphs below. Then do the exercises that follow.

I

Weekends

Weekends are more important for me in Egypt than weekends in the United States. In Egypt, I usually go to my father's ranch which is about fifty miles from where I live in Cairo. There I usually do physical work which I miss in my work at the university. <u>I also go swimming in the lake close to our ranch.</u> In the evening, I go back to Cairo where I meet all my brothers and sisters. <u>We eat dinner with our parents in my older brother's home.</u> After dinner, we stay until late to discuss our personal problems and also to discuss the solutions. <u>The evening is a good time for our children to play together and to become close to each other.</u> That is important for all Egyptian families. <u>In contrast, my weekends in the United States are more lonely and more boring than they were in Egypt.</u> I usually study for my classes, go to the supermarket, and spend some of the day with my Egyptian friends in the Muslim meeting hall. When I have time, I drive to Seattle, and I sometimes telephone my brother in Houston. My weekends in Egypt were certainly better than my weekends in the United States, but I hope that after enough time my weekends here will be as beautiful as my weekends in my country.

Khadr Hassan
Egypt

____ EXERCISE 8K _____

1. Put parentheses around 4 comparative adjectives.
2. Put brackets around 2 time clauses.
3. Identify the subject (S) and the verb (V) in each of the underlined sentences.
4. Circle the comparison structure in the last sentence.

II

Weekends in Tunisia and in the United States

Like American students, Tunisians practice various activities on the weekends to enjoy themselves, but these activities _____ different from one country to the other because the two cultures are different. In fact, American students can make dates with their girlfriends to spend the weekend together. However, it is not polite in Tunisia to go with a girlfriend without marriage. In many other ways, however, students in both countries spend weekends in almost the same way. For example, both Tunisian and U.S. students can go on picnics, on trips to the mountains, or to other scenic places. Some _____ to go to the movies or to play electronic games. Other students spend their weekends in various clubs such as musical or dramatic clubs. Still others _____ the habit of going to a stadium every Sunday to watch matches or to play games like soccer and hockey. There are other students in both Tunisia and the United States who _____ their weekends studying and preparing their assignments. Finally, many students _____ home every weekend to see their friends and relatives.

VERBS: be   drive   have   prefer   spend

Zaher Rebai
Tunisia

—— EXERCISE 8L ————————————————————

1. Write the correct present tense verbs in the blanks. Use each verb on the list only once.
2. Underline 5 comparison or contrast structures in the paragraph.
3. Circle 5 infinitive verbs.
4. Put parentheses around the connectors in the paragraph. Identify them as additional information OR contrasting information OR cause-effect information connectors.

III

Weekends Here and There

Weekends in my country, Kenya, are different than in the U.S. I have been in the U.S. for a month. When Friday approaches, I think of how I will spend another boring weekend. I always have three activities on the weekend: washing my clothes, reading the newspapers, and doing my homework. Usually by Saturday afternoon I have finished these activities. The remaining one-and-a-half days I spend by reading other books, magazines, and newspapers, or by walking up and down in my room, or by watching TV. My room directly faces the main street, so I keep on counting the number of cars passing on Plum Street. Oh! What a boring weekend! <u>Back home, Kenyan weekends are special days</u>. By Friday afternoon, one can tell by the smiles on the faces that the weekend is at the door: two good days of visiting friends, going to the movies, and traveling to national parks. Many of us also think that the weekend is a good time to be with our animals, dipping, inoculating, and treating the sick animals, and counting the newborn and total number of the flock to learn whether any goats have been lost. Taking the animals to an open grassland, and watching them gripping grass between their jaws, makes me elated. Caring for the small lambs is another exciting adventure. When the lambs arrive at the green pastures, one can tell that Silas has had a good weekend by the way he stands, one leg across the other, the spear leaning against the shoulder, the sword hanging at his waist, and two sticks in his hands. <u>He whistles to communicate with his flock</u>.

Silas Parsitau
Kenya

1. Put brackets around at least 10 prepositional phrases.
2. Identify the subject (S) and the verb (V) in the underlined sentences.
3. Circle 7 adjectives in the paragraph.
4. Put parentheses around the contrast structure in the first sentence.

____ **WRITING ASSIGNMENT** _____

Find a photograph of yourself as a child. Compare the person in that photograph with the person you are now. Answer some of the questions below:

Where were you when the photograph was taken?

How old were you?

What were you doing just before the photograph was taken?

How are you different now?

How are you the same?

Use comparison and contrast structures in your paragraph. Use comparative adjectives and appropriate connectors.

> There is no ivory with a flaw.
>
> translated by
> *Hadi Pasaribu*

____ **WRITING ASSIGNMENT** _____

Study the chart below. It shows the results of a survey of 807 U.S. television viewers. Write a paragraph describing the chart. Answer some of the questions below:

What does the chart tell you about U.S. television viewing habits? (probably)

Do you agree with the survey? How are your views similar? How are they different?

Why do you think North Americans prefer some kinds of programs and dislike others?

As you write, plan your paragraph. Use some of these structures:

> According to . . . ,
>
> Most North Americans (*XX* percent) . . .
>
> Other Americans regularly watch . . .
>
> Some Americans (*XX* percent) like . . .
>
> In my opinion, . . .

SURVEY OF U.S. TELEVISION WATCHING HABITS

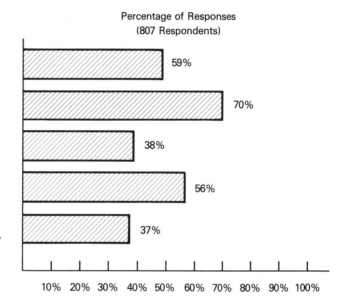

Survey Statements	Percentage of Responses (807 Respondents)
I am watching the same number of hours of television this year as I did last year.	59%
The news programs on television are better now than they were five years ago.	70%
The regular network prime-time television programs are better now than they were five years ago.	38%
The overall quality of television is the same now as it was five years ago.	56%
The overall quality of television is worse now than it was five years ago.	37%

10% 20% 30% 40% 50% 60% 70% 80% 90% 100%

Exchange paragraphs with a classmate:

> A. Read the paragraph.
>
> B. Underline the comparative adjectives.
>
> C. Put parentheses around the time clauses. Circle the time words.
>
> D. Underline any errors in the paragraph. Discuss these errors with your classmate.

OTHER PARAGRAPH TOPICS

Dinner in My Country vs. Dinner in the United States (or another country)

How I Am Similar to

> a diamond ring
>
> a soccer game
>
> a camel

a detective novel

a pizza

???????????

Teachers in My Country vs. Teachers in the United States (or another country)

Traffic in My Country vs. Traffic in the United States (or another country)

A Childhood Belief vs. the Reality of Adulthood

WRITING PROJECTS

Individual Project

Write several paragraphs about your education in your country. Include paragraphs about some of the topics below:

The Primary Education System in My Country

My Favorite Primary School Memory

My Best Primary School Teacher

An Adjustment I Made in Primary School

An Unforgettable Primary School Experience

My Best Friend in Primary School

The Secondary School System in My Country

My Favorite Class (Teacher, Subject) in Secondary School

Sports in My Secondary School

My Favorite Sport in Secondary School

A Terrible Experience in Secondary School

My Graduation from Secondary School

Gather these paragraphs into a booklet. Illustrate the booklet with photographs, drawings, and documents from the school(s) you attended. Present the booklet to a local public school for use in their classes.

Group Project

Make a survey about television viewing habits like the one on page 211. Ask students NOT in your class to complete the survey. Then compile the survey data, and summarize the data in chart form and in paragraph form. Post the results of the survey on your classroom bulletin board, and make copies of the results for the students who participated in the survey. Send the results of the survey to a local television station with some suggestions for changes in programming.

TELEVISION VIEWING SURVEY

Please read the questions below and answer them.

1. Do you watch television? Yes _____   No _____

2. How many hours do you watch each week?

   1–5 _____   7–12 _____   13–20 _____   more than 20 _____

3. What programs do you watch often?

   news programs _____   game shows _____   dramas _____

   movies _____   sports _____   police shows _____

   other (specify) _____

4. Which programs are similar to programs you watch in your country?

   _____

5. Which programs are different from programs you watch in your country?

   _____

6. How are they different?

   _____

   _____

7. What are your three favorite programs?

   A. _____

   B. _____

   C. _____

8. What kinds of programs do you dislike most?

   _____

   _____

9. Why?

   _____

   _____

10. What advice would you give U.S. television producers about U.S. television?

    _____

    _____

Appendix A

Some Regular and Irregular English Verbs*

Root form	Third person singular	Past Regular	Irregular	Special verbs
admit	admits	admitted		
agree	agrees	agreed		
become	becomes		became	
begin	begins		began	
bite	bites		bit	
blow	blows		blew	
break	breaks		broke	
bring	brings		brought	
build	builds		built	
buy	buys		bought	
catch	catches		caught	
choose	chooses		chose	
come	comes		came	
cost	costs		cost	
cut	cuts		cut	

*NOTE: See the spelling rules on the inside front cover of this textbook.

Root form	Third person singular	Past Regular	Irregular	Special verbs	(cont.)
dance	dances	danced			
dial	dials	dialed			
do	does		did		
draw	draws		drew		
drink	drinks		drank		
drive	drives		drove		
earn	earns	earned			
eat	eats		ate		
end	ends	ended			
enjoy	enjoys	enjoyed			
enter	enters	entered			
excuse	excuses	excused			
fall	falls		fell		
feed	feeds		fed		
feel	feels		felt		
fight	fights		fought		
fill	fills	filled			
find	finds		found		
finish	finishes	finished			
flow	flows	flowed			
fly	flies		flew		
follow	follows	followed			
forget	forgets		forgot		
forgive	forgives		forgave		
get	gets		got		
give	gives		gave		
go	goes		went		
grow	grows		grew		
hang	hangs		hung		
happen	happens	happened			
have	has		had	have to	
hear	hears		heard		
help	helps	helped			
hope	hopes	hoped			
hurry	hurries	hurried			
hurt	hurts		hurt		
include	includes	included			
interview	interviews	interviewed			
jump	jumps	jumped			
keep	keeps		kept		
kill	kills	killed			
knock	knocks	knocked			
know	knows		knew		
land	lands	landed			
laugh	laughs	laughed			
learn	learns	learned			
lift	lifts	lifted			
like	likes	liked			
listen	listens	listened		listen to	
live	lives	lived			
look	looks	looked			
lose	loses		lost		
make	makes		made		

| Root form | Third person singular | Past | | Special verbs | (cont.) |
		Regular	Irregular		
manage	manages	managed			
mean	means		meant		
meet	meets		met		
miss	misses	missed			
move	moves	moved			
need	needs	needed		need to	
offer	offers	offered			
open	opens	opened			
order	orders	ordered			
park	parks	parked			
pay	pays		paid		
pick	picks	picked			
play	plays	played			
prefer	prefers	preferred			
put	puts		put		
rain	rains	rained			
read	reads		read		
remember	remembers	remembered			
request	requests	requested			
return	returns	returned			
ride	rides		rode		
run	runs		ran		
say	says		said		
see	sees		saw		
sell	sells		sold		
send	sends		sent		
serve	serves	served			
shake	shakes		shook		
share	shares	shared			
shine	shines		shone		
sign	signs	signed			
sing	sings		sang		
sit	sits		sat		
sleep	sleeps		slept		
smile	smiles	smiled			
smoke	smokes	smoked			
snow	snows	snowed			
speak	speaks		spoke		
spell	spells	spelled			
spend	spends		spent		
stand	stands		stood		
start	starts	started			
stay	stays	stayed			
stop	stops	stopped			
study	studies	studied			
take	takes		took		
talk	talks	talked			
teach	teaches		taught		
tell	tells		told		
thank	thanks	thanked			
think	thinks		thought		
throw	throws		threw		

Root form	Third person singular	Past Regular	Past Irregular	Special verbs	*(cont.)*
travel	travels	traveled			
turn	turns	turned			
type	types	typed			
understand	understands		understood		
use	uses	used		used to	
visit	visits	visited			
wait	waits	waited			
wake	wakes		woke		
walk	walks	walked			
want	wants	wanted		wanted to	
watch	watches	watched			
wear	wears		wore		
win	wins		won		
work	works	worked			
worry	worries	worried			
write	writes		wrote		

Appendix B

Some English Adjectives and Adverbs**

Root form	-er/more than	-est/the most	Adverb
angry	angrier	angriest	angrily
bad	worse*	worst*	badly
beautiful	more beautiful	most beautiful	beautifully
big	bigger	biggest	_____
busy	busier	busiest	busily
careless	more careless	most careless	carelessly
comfortable	more comfortable	most comfortable	comfortably
confusing	more confusing	most confusing	confusingly
convenient	more convenient	most convenient	conveniently
easy	easier	easiest	easily
expensive	more expensive	most expensive	expensively
fast	faster	fastest	fast*
frustrating	more frustrating	most frustrating	_____
good	better*	best*	good*
happy	happier	happiest	happily

*Irregular forms

**NOTE: See the spelling rules in Appendix C on page 218.

Root form	-er/more than	-est/the most	Adverb (cont.)
hard	harder	hardest	hard*
hot	hotter	hottest	_____
important	more important	most important	importantly
intelligent	more intelligent	most intelligent	intelligently
interesting	more interesting	most interesting	interestingly
large	larger	largest	_____
late	later	latest	_____
lazy	lazier	laziest	lazily
long	longer	longest	_____
noisy	noisier	noisiest	noisily
old	older	oldest	_____
pretty	prettier	prettiest	prettily
quiet	quieter	quietest	quietly
serious	more serious	most serious	seriously
small	smaller	smallest	_____
soft	softer	softest	softly
strong	stronger	strongest	strongly
successful	more successful	most successful	successfully
tall	taller	tallest	
terrible	more terrible	most terrible	terribly
useful	more useful	most useful	usefully
warm	warmer	warmest	warmly

Appendix C

Spelling Rules for English Adjectives

End of Word	Example	-er Ending	-est Ending	Comments
-e	*white*	whit*er**	whit*est**	*Add -r or -st.
	larg*e*	larg*er*	larg*est*	
2 consonants	da*rk*	dark*er*	dark*est*	Regular forms.
	o*ld*	old*er*	old*est*	
1 vowel + 1 consonant	th*in*	thin*ner**	thin*nest**	*One-syllable adjective: double final consonant.
	b*ig*	big*ger**	big*gest**	
	qui*et*	quiet*er*	quiet*est*	*Two-syllable adjective with stress on first syllable: do not double final consonant.
1 consonant + *y*	hea*vy*	heav*ier**	heav*iest**	*Drop the *y*; add -ies or -ied.
	ea*sy*	eas*ier**	eas*iest**	
	pret*ty*	prett*ier**	prett*iest*	

Index

P

Paragraph form, 15
Past continuous verbs, 153
  spelling of, *inside front cover*
Planning strategies
  charts, 18, 45, 90, 112, 148–49,
    174–75, 181–82, 194
  listing, 50, 87, 148–49
  questions, 10, 22, 24, 32, 35, 39,
    66, 72, 93, 97, 128, 140–41,
    153, 199, 208
  sentence structures, 93, 124, 125,
    183, 193, 198, 209
  trees, 102–3, 171, 204
Poem. *See* Lionrise
Possessive adjectives, 5
Prepositional phrases, 57, 68
Prepositions
  of place, 56–57
  of time, 67
Present continuous verbs, 149
  spelling of, *inside front cover*
Present tense verbs, 28–29
  negative, 48
  spelling of, *inside front cover*, 32
Pronouns
  object pronouns, 9
  subject pronouns, 9

Q

Questionnaires
  housing, 184–85
  television, 211
Questions, 7
Questions (planning strategy), 10, 22,
    24, 32, 35, 39, 66, 72, 93, 97,
    128, 140–41, 153, 166, 182,
    199, 208

R

Regular verbs, list of, 212–15

S

Sentence structures (planning
    strategy), 93, 124, 125, 183,
    193, 198, 209
, so, 94
Special verbs

hear/listen, 141
say/tell, 141
see/look, 141
Special verbs, list of, 212–15
Spelling
  general rules, *inside front cover*
  past tense, irregular verbs, 113
  past tense, regular verbs, 106
  present tense verbs, 32
  rules for adjectives, 218
Subject pronouns, 9
Subject-verb agreement, 71
Subject-verb-complement, 13
Surveys. *See* Questionnaires

T

There is/there are, 35
Time clauses
  after . . ., 184
  before . . . ., 184
  when . . . ., 184
Time prepositions, 67
To be, 2
  negative, 46
To have, 4
  negative, 46
Too/very, 144
Trees (planning strategy), 102–3,
    171, 204

U

Used to, 167–68

V

Verbs
  of feeling + adjectives, 116
  imperatives, 91
  infinitives, 162
  list of, 212–15
  negative
    infinitives, 163
    past tense, 119
    regular verbs, 48
    to be, 46
    to have, 46
  past continuous, 153
  present continuous, 149
  present tense, 28–29
  special verbs, 141

3297